Pr‹
on the

MW00770713

In *On the Other Side*, Julie Jacky courageously and transparently shares her deeply personal traumas and triumphs. Witnessing her profound evolution has been my honor, and I invite you to find yourself in her impactful story so you too can experience profound healing. This book is a true gem.

—Nancy Levin
bestselling author of
Setting Boundaries Will Set You Free

In *On the Other Side,* Julie Jacky gets personal and specific about how to heal the crippling effects of childhood sexual abuse. Her persistence and courage in her own healing process show us what it really takes, and as she experiences her breakthrough into the lightness and freedom that come with true forgiveness, we want to celebrate her triumph—as well as fearlessly face any of our own bad stories and be done with them. Julie's writing style is friendly and goes down easy, and this book will be so helpful to many people. Thank you, Julie!

—Mary Hayes Grieco
author of *Unconditional Forgiveness:
A Simple and Proven Method to
Forgive Everyone and Everything*

You won't want to put this powerful book down. *On the Other Side* is truly an inspiration, and is deeply relatable for all readers whether you have experienced sexual abuse or not. It is raw and real and provides heartfelt hope for all who have been through any kind of trauma or sexual abuse in their lives. The incredible hard work Julie went through to heal from her past shows us that we too can all do the hard work; we can all heal wounds that we once thought couldn't be healed. We can all take our spiritual, mental, emotional, and physical health into our own hands and heal ourselves.

—Dr. Angela Elliot DC, CACCP
pediatric and family chiropractor

As Julie courageously opens her heart and shares her journey through healing her past, we see that healing is possible for us too. Her stories confirm for us that our past does not have to define us nor dictate our future; we can indeed find peace within ourselves and realize that we are truly enough. Julie's must-read memoir is a convincing invitation to do our personal work. Let's begin.

—Ann Kerr Romberg
certified life and horse-guided coach,
author of several e-books that help
coaches support people on their journeys

ON THE OTHER SIDE

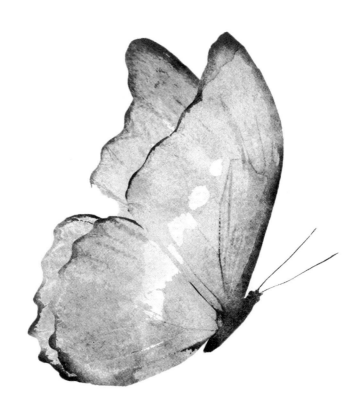

on the other side

a spiritual memoir

julie jacky

Minneapolis

This book is a memoir and it reflects my present recollections of experiences in my life over time. I recognize that others' memories of events described in this book may be different than my own. Some names and identifying details have been changed to protect the privacy of individuals as this book is not intended to hurt anyone. Some events have been compressed and some dialogue has been recreated.

"The Other Side" © 2017 Chara Rodriguera

ISBN 13: 978-1-63489-330-5

Library of Congress Catalog Number: 2020905043
Printed in the United States of America
First Printing: 2020

24   23   22   21   20   5   4   3   2   1

Cover design by Emily Mahon
Interior design by Patrick Maloney

Wise Ink Creative Publishing
807 Broadway St NE
Suite 46
Minneapolis, MN, 55413

To order, visit www.itascabooks.com or call 1-800-901-3480.
Reseller discounts available.

For all who have whispered *me too*

THE OTHER SIDE

by Chara Rodriguera

It must look so simple
from the outside,
from the other side,

but for me
it's not so easy.

My steps
have become
frozen.

It feels as though
I'm stuck in concrete,

locked in a cage
that
I
have
chosen.

I can't see past my fears.

I can't see through my tears.

I can't believe
it's been
so
many
years.

I could wallow
and wait.

I could blame
and hate.

I could continue
to repress
who I am
and not
address
or express
what I feel
and what is real
and what I need
to heal.

But,
I will always know
deep inside
that the one

who holds
the key
is
me.

The key is to shift
what I see.

The key
is to
breathe
deeply
and
free.

The key is to
love me

love me

love me

to the

other side

because I deserve

to be

happy.

Contents

Introduction   1

Part One: Facing the Past
1. The Courage to Be Vulnerable   9
2. Whack-a-Mole   31
3. Digging Deep   43
4. Digging in Deeper   55
5. Impact   65
6. The Mind-Body Connection   77

Part Two: Finding My Voice
7. Worthy   91
8. Line in the Sand   101
9. Speaking Up   119
10. Christmas in July   133
11. Forgiveness Is a Process   149

Part Three: Healing for the Future
12. The Message in Meditation   171
13. Out of My Head and Into My Heart   183
14. The Storm   199
15. Anonymous   215
16. The Work Continues   239
17. Letter to Reader   259

Resources   263
Mentors Who Helped Me   265
Gratitude   269
About the Author   273

INTRODUCTION

Dan chased me from three houses down the street, all the way to my home. *I'll be safe once I get inside*, I thought. *He isn't going to touch me there.*

Almost all the other times Dan had touched me over the past six years had been in or around his home, not mine. I didn't think he would actually enter my home and abuse me there.

I ran down the fourteen long cement steps and could feel my heart pounding in my chest each time my foot hit the ground. When I got to my house, I opened the screen door and the front wooden door, hurried inside, and pushed the wooden door shut with the weight of my body as quickly as I could. Shaking, my fingers reached for the deadbolt to move it into the lock position. Before I could click it into place, Dan shoved his body up against the other side of the door so hard that it pushed me back. It opened enough for him to insert his foot between the frame and the door. I couldn't shut it. He was too strong for me.

Out of desperation, and still thinking Dan wouldn't enter my home, I stopped pushing on the door, quickly turned my body in the other direction, and ran to the bedroom. He was faster than me and shoved his foot into that doorway too.

"Stop!" I screamed. "Leave me alone! You have a girlfriend. Go touch her. Not me!"

1

I don't know if I will ever forget Dan's reply: "I need to practice on you." As if I were some blow-up doll.

I was in shock. It happened so fast. I don't remember how Dan knocked me to the floor and pinned my upper body against the wall near the bedroom door. If I moved, it hurt worse. My lower body was naked and splayed out on the floor. My skirt was up, my underwear shoved off to the side. My legs were spread apart enough for him to do what he wanted. I could feel his heavy breath on my privates. I closed my eyes to block it out. Then I felt his tongue touch me. My body cringed, and I pushed my eyelids down tighter to keep the tears in as he practiced on me.

Then, from outside the house, I heard a rapid pounding sound getting louder, the click of the metal door handle, and a quick squeak of the door spring. My eyes opened wide. I gasped and stopped breathing in hopes that no one would hear or see me. All of a sudden, someone flew past the bedroom door and rushed into the bathroom. It was my stepdad. The bathroom door slammed shut. My heart pounded through my chest.

Dan got off me and stood up faster than my stepdad had run by. He apologized to me—for the first time ever. I got up off the floor and pulled my skirt down. He promised he would never touch me ever again if I didn't tell on him. Then he ran out of the house.

My stepdad was still in the bathroom, and my heart was still pounding. You'd think I would have felt relief that it was finally over, after six years of enduring abuse whenever Dan had seen fit, but my body was shaking in fear. I didn't know if my stepdad had seen anything. I didn't know what he'd say to me. I was scared that I would get in trouble, as if *I* had done something wrong. I didn't want him to think Dan was my boy-friend, but I also feared my stepdad would beat the fucking shit out of Dan if he knew what had really happened.

When my stepdad came out of the bathroom, he didn't say a word. Neither did I.

It was finally over, but not really.

For well over twenty-five years, I minimized the abuse be-cause Dan hadn't penetrated me with his penis. I thought I was fine, that I didn't need therapy, help, or anything of the sort. It wasn't until I was in my early forties, when I took an online EFT (Emotional Freedom Technique, or tapping) course on weight loss and body confidence, that I realized I needed to get help.

Once I sought help, I developed awareness after aware-ness of how sexual abuse had permeated every aspect of my life, including my health and especially my relationships. I was afraid of conflict, afraid of speaking up, afraid of sharing my opinion, and afraid of saying no. I always kept myself busy and was a proud overachiever. I was unable to relax because my body was still in fight-flight-freeze mode, trying to keep me safe.

As I worked through those aspects of the sexual abuse, my life began to transform for the better. I forgave my abuser, made peace with my divorce, and strengthened my relation-ships. Now I'm living life on my own terms.

Sadly, as you may know, sexual abuse is an experience shared by far too many women. It takes place everywhere and occurs when we don't expect it. It's also one of society's worst best-kept secrets. We'd rather stick our heads in the sand and pretend it doesn't exist so we don't have to talk about it or deal with it. But that stops us from living life wholly and keeps the worst secrets buried, perpetuating the cycle of abuse.

I think that's all starting to shift now, because those of us who experienced abuse are learning we can empower ourselves. We can get help and stop allowing our past to haunt us and dictate our future. When we open up and let out the embarrassing secrets we've kept buried, our lives transform and unfold in seemingly magical ways. And by opening up, we also contribute to healing society and stopping the abuse cycle.

On the Other Side is about my healing and forgiveness journey. My stories are personal, deep, and uninhibited. You'll find them shared in three parts. The first section focuses on facing the past and becoming aware of the impact the abuse had on my life. The second part is about finding my voice and letting go. The third part is about healing for the future by completely redesigning my life into one I love. Each chapter revolves around healing from my past and taking responsibility for my life. This book isn't about blaming or wanting to prosecute anyone. It's not an angry "I hate men" or "I hate anyone else" book. It's my personal story, from my experience, about my journey. It's intended to help others start or continue the healing process on their journey.

If you too are a sexual abuse survivor, I hope that, through my stories, you'll become aware of how sexual abuse has kept you stuck in your past and affected your health, your relationships with others, and—most importantly—your relationship with yourself. Take your time with reading it. Give yourself breaks so you can reflect on what is coming up for you. Write in a journal. Go for walks. Do what you need to do to take care of yourself. As you continue reading, you'll be inspired to finally open up, seek help, and move forward on your healing journey.

Frankly, the healing and forgiveness process after childhood sexual abuse isn't easy or fun. It can be an excruciatingly painful emotional excavation. But please don't let that stop you. Although the abuse wasn't my fault and isn't yours either, it is our responsibility to overcome the pain and change our lives.

It's up to us to take our own power back. It's up to us to stop saying yes to shit we don't want to do but think we should do. It's up to us to say yes to the things we dream or get excited about but keep telling ourselves we shouldn't for rational or logical reasons. It's up to us to put ourselves first instead of last, since we don't have time or energy left after taking care of everyone else. It's up to us to draw a line in the sand and decide when enough is enough. Life needs to change—now. Commit to doing what it takes to make those changes, even when they're hard.

What's the alternative? You could stay in a life you don't totally love. Or continue to feel like something is missing. Or keep searching for the next product or service that might make you happy. But you don't really want these options anymore, do you?

So what's the reward for making these changes? Freedom! Freedom awaits you on the other side of digging in to heal your past.

Let's keep reading.

—Julie Jacky

PART ONE

facing
the past

Chapter One

THE COURAGE TO BE VULNERABLE

ONE TRUE SENTENCE

I was sitting on the edge of a black, velvety theater chair, looking up on the stage from the second row of the dimly lit Sherwood Auditorium in La Jolla, California. It felt like my heart was enlarging and blossoming open as each speaker, one by one, pulled me into a significant and emotional turning point in their life with just "one true sentence." On the first day of the Personal Story Power workshop, Bo Eason, a former NFL player, acclaimed Broadway playwright and performer, and international story coach, had guided us through some writing exercises. We were a group of small business entrepreneurs who were looking to make a difference in the world and grow our businesses by connecting with others in a meaningful way. It was time to share those stories. I wiped a tear from the side of my eye.

Oh, wow, I thought. *These people are sharing intimate and painful secrets from their lives that people don't usually share. I want to know more about their stories. They are going for it. They are all so confident. I can't go up onstage and share this lame-ass story. I gotta hurry up and pick a more vulnerable one before my row gets called up there.*

I closed my eyes, took a deep breath in, and slowly let it out.

Although two stories popped into my mind, I knew which story I needed to share. I had jotted notes about the story in my black hardcover Personal Story Power journal the day before. It was a story I had never shared with anyone before because I felt too ashamed and embarrassed to tell anyone. But during that low moment in my life, I had promised myself I would never, ever, ever be in that position again. I was proud of all the changes I had made in my life since then, and I was pleased I was keeping the promise to myself. I figured, despite my nerves, it was an excellent opportunity to open up and share because I was in a safe space where others were doing the same.

Plus, at that point, I thought it would be more embarrassing to not get vulnerable in my sharing, even though I was still nervous.

Oh God, what am I doing? I questioned. *Please help me be able to share this onstage.*

I quickly grabbed a pink gel pen out of my pencil pouch, put my journal on my lap, flipped open to the next blank page, and nervously scribbled out my embarrassing story about being broke. I distilled it down into one true sentence. When I felt satisfied with my sentence, I wrote it out on a light yellow Post-it note; tapped the arm of one of my dearest friends, Kim, who was sitting next to me; and gave her the note to read. She read it, looked me in the eye, and gave me a nod and a thumbs-up to let me know it was good.

I practiced the sentence over and over in my head until my group was called up for our opportunity onstage. There were about twenty of us who stood up and filed out of the first two rows of auditorium chairs. We walked up the stairs and onto the stage platform, where we lined up in a row in front of the long black curtain hanging from the back of the stage. One at a time, each person stepped forward to deliver their "one true sentence" to the audience. I waited to go last so I could hear what each person shared and attentively listen to the feedback Bo gave each of them in order to learn from it and use it during my sentence delivery.

It felt like slow motion as the second-to-last lady exited across the front of the stage and down the stairs to head back to her seat. I was next. The last time I had been on an auditorium stage was in eighth grade, when I played an alto saxophone duet with my buddy Matt. We had both been so nervous that we laughed most of the way through it. This time, although I was equally anxious, I knew I wouldn't laugh, and I was hoping I wouldn't cry or die from embarrassment. I was afraid that my workshop friends wouldn't know what to say to me after what I was about to share with them. But I needed to deliver this message with confidence, no matter how my body and mind continued to react.

Walk confidently, Julie, I encouraged myself. *Holy crap, my palms are sweaty. You can do this, Julie. You can do this. Just remember to look out at one person in the audience and hold the pause at the end. You've got this.*

The heaviness of the anxiety in my chest made it hard to breathe in, but I pushed air down to my belly to summon up courage on my exhale. I stepped forward, all the way up to the front center of the stage, hoping no one could see my legs quivering. I paused.

I stood still, with my toes at the edge of the stage. I looked out into the audience and, although I knew over 100 people were staring at me, I couldn't see most of them.

I held back the tears I felt welling up and locked eyes with

Kim, who was back sitting in the second row. I spoke as if I were having a conversation with just her and no one else in the room. "When I was thirty-eight, I took money out of my son's savings account, to keep the lights on." I heard the audience gasp and stood in silence.

Although I felt like I wanted to run off the stage as fast as I could to hide in a corner somewhere, I forced myself to continue standing there in silence to let the audience take it in, just as Bo had instructed us to do.

Julie, wait, I reminded myself. *Wait. Hold the pause. Hold the pause a little longer. You're almost done.*

I didn't know if anyone could hear the loud beating of my heart like I could, or if they could see the sweat I felt seeping through to the armpits of my shirt. I'm sure I was holding my breath too. As a single tear slowly rolled down my right cheek, I let out an audible sigh, and I looked over at Bo for approval. "Was that long enough?"

He looked squarely into my eyes from the side of the stage and said, "Julie, did you see what you did to the audience?"

Deflecting my nervousness with humor like I tended to do, I let Bo know I couldn't see a damn thing with those bright lights.

"Julie, you had them gasping. You can do anything with them and take them anywhere now. They want to know what happens next, how you got yourself out of that situation and ended up onstage sharing your story. They will follow your every word."

I felt good about delivering my message, and more tears that felt like relief and freedom welled up behind my eyes. I exited the stage, sat down in my chair, and silently took in what had just happened.

I couldn't believe I had just shared that story. I actually felt relief. My body felt lighter.

I guess that's what "the truth shall see you free" feels like, I thought.

Bill, a fellow workshop groupie I had first met at Brendon Burchard's High Performance Academy a couple of years earlier, came up to me at the break and told me how much he admired me for what I had gone through. I wondered how he could be so inspired by my story, which seemed so insignificant compared to his own amazing story. Onstage he appeared as if he had healed from the anger and pain of being wrongfully locked up in a mental institution for years after his brother, who had set their home on fire, blamed him. This had happened not once, but two different times. I was in awe as he stood tall and calmly shared his story without anger or resentment in his voice. He inspired me to want to be a better person and forgive people who had harmed me in the past.

Bill said he could see I was nervous by the expression on my face and the stiffness in my shoulders that I didn't realize had shown. With soft eyes, he looked at me, bent down, wrapped his arms around me, and gave me a big, warm hug. He said he was happy to know me.

Joanne, a lady whom I also recognized from other workshops, approached me. I looked her up and down, took a deep breath in, and held it, uncertain of what she'd say to me. We had met the prior spring at Brendon Burchard's World's Greatest Speaker event and again that fall at his 10x event. We hadn't connected personally. I quietly stood with the different groups of people, admiring how well-put-together she appeared every time I saw her both weekends. Each strand of golden-brown hair was in perfect place, and her beautiful smile showcased her perfectly aligned, glistening white teeth. I had never known what to say to her before because I was intimidated by her appearance. She dressed so well; I thought she must be very successful in her online women's empowerment business. We didn't talk much because I figured she probably didn't want to talk to someone like me who owned a small, insignificant jewelry business, especially since I was closing it.

But after she walked up to me, she said, "Julie, I don't mean this in a bad way, but I always felt you were very standoffish at other events, and now I feel connected to you because you were so authentic up there. I haven't told many people this before, but I've struggled financially too." I let out a breath, and my shoulders relaxed in relief.

What? She struggled financially too? I wondered. *Huh. I'm stunned. I feel like I can talk with her now, knowing she's struggled in life too.*

As I connected with others in the group, I was amazed that having the courage to be vulnerable by opening up and sharing that difficult time in my life pulled people in closer. I mulled through this dichotomy in my mind.

Well, clearly, I didn't die after standing on that stage and revealing that part of myself to others. My friends weren't afraid to talk to me. Quite the opposite. I have a stronger bond with these friends now. We connected in a deeper and more meaningful way because we shared one true sentence from a super tough time in our lives. I understand what Bo meant by "vulnerability is strength." I feel stronger and more confident.

The truth is, we all have painful and deeply distressing experiences that turn out to be a blessing. They help shape our lives and offer us the opportunity to help others who are going through similar challenges.

Up until this point, I had tried not to think about the moment I had just shared. It had been at least six years since the troubled financial time when my life spiraled out of control. I had gotten laid off from my job and worked endless hours building my two businesses: jewelry and travel. But I hadn't been making ends meet very well, even though I pretended I was just fine. I put a happy mask on with the biggest fucking fake smile plastered across my face I could muster as I slowly drained my retirement account to pay the bills. I focused on being positive and acted as if everything was A-OK, because that's what I understood the Law of Attraction and "fake it 'til you make it" to mean. But the façade came slamming down not long after the stock market crashed in 2008. Eventually, after swallowing my pride, I ended up filing for bankruptcy, and it was that exact moment that I vowed to myself I would never be in that position again. I started digging in and learning how to change my money mindset by immersing myself in teachings from the late Dr. Wayne Dyer, Abraham Hicks, and the late Louise Hay. The lessons were about changing my thinking. I listened to them on CD, DVD, and YouTube as many hours a day as I possibly could so they would soak in. Within eighteen months of filing for bankruptcy, I started earning six figures.

But then I had a new problem. I was making more money than I ever had before, and I was afraid I would make the same mistakes. I decided once again to do what I do best, which is immerse myself in learning. But this time, it was on how to manage my money best.

Back in my seat after break, my body began to loosen its death grip on that secret it had held tightly for years. My neck and shoulders felt looser and lighter. Overall, I felt happier and freer. All this was simply because I had shared my truth and stopped letting shame and embarrassment control me.

At the end of the workshop, Bo asked participants to share what had shifted inside them after their onstage experience. For me, I realized I still carried emotional baggage around other things in my past that I needed to face.

Man, I thought, *if I feel this much better after sharing that turbulent financial time with people, then I can only imagine how I might feel after I deal with the other crap from my past that I've hidden. Fuck!*

I hated to admit this, but I now understood even more that I needed to deal with other painful memories: the haunting sexual abuse scenes I had been ignoring for years. I didn't want to have to divulge out loud to the therapist that someone had touched me so many times. As an adult, I felt stupid and as if I should have known better and stopped it from repeatedly happening. I didn't want to tell even one more person that I had never told anyone at the time it was happening. Because when they asked why I didn't tell anyone, their chastising tone of judgment pierced my heart. I felt unable to defend my eleven-year-old self's decision. Even though I'd rather not have to talk about sexual abuse ever again, it was essential to work through it to feel freedom on the other side. It was a good thing I had another appointment booked with the therapist when I got back home.

OVERACHIEVER

Just two years before that onstage experience, my life looked very different. I was a lot more stressed and frequently didn't feel very well. In the mornings, I tried to pop out of bed at the first alarm instead of hitting the snooze button, but I didn't seem to have enough energy. I knew from experience that exercising in the morning not only jump-started my day but also gave me extra energy that lasted all day. I wanted to feel that again, but I couldn't seem to get up early to do some kind of workout before getting ready for the day. That bothered me. It was a big contrast to several years earlier, when I was training to run a marathon. Back then, I got up early and ran between five to fourteen miles before starting work at 8:00 a.m. Now, I worried if I was getting an illness or even a disease like cancer because I was so low-energy. I quickly brushed those thoughts of illness out of my mind as quickly as they came in.

I don't know why I can't get out of bed and get my ass to the gym to lose this fricking weight, I thought. *I did it before. It seemed so much easier to get out of bed then, but now . . . it feels like I have a migraine hangover behind my eyes, and I have to fight just to open them.*

If I can't get a full-hour workout in, it just isn't worth the trouble, I reasoned. I laid my head back down on the pillow for "just five more minutes," even though I wanted to sleep another full hour or three. Unable to drift back to sleep with the pre-sunrise light glistening ever so slightly in between the Venetian blinds, my mind wandered with frustration.

Despite hearing the voice of Brendon Burchard, one of my mentors, say, *"Don't let other people's agendas dictate your day"* in my head, I scrunched my eyes to shield them from the bright light and looked at my email on my cell phone before I got out of bed. *How can there be so many emails in my inbox already? It's only 5:30 a.m.!*

I immediately felt overwhelmed and told myself I needed

to get up to leave for work as soon as possible. I wanted to avoid rush-hour traffick and put out the latest work fire ASAP. (Yes, I spelled *traffick* correctly. Everyone else forgets to put the letter *k* on the end to emphasize the *ick* part.) Not wanting to waste time sitting in traffick was the only thing that stopped me from replying to the emails right then and motivated me to get up.

I was vice president at a small family office and was my boss's go-to person as well as the manager of human resources, the office, and the employees. It was my job to know everything that was going on at all times and keep the projects moving.

When I first started at the family office, I quickly learned how it's different than a family business. The sole purpose of a family office is to serve a wealthy family and be stewards for them. Being a steward means watching out for them, taking care of them by providing excellent service each day, and putting time on their side.

The easiest way I have learned to explain this to others is by having them picture it in their mind. I asked them to imagine, if you will, that you have an abundance of money that allows you to employ others to help manage your life so you can spend time focusing on what you want to do. You have someone to clean your home, run errands, and grocery shop for you. You have another person to take care of your home and yard maintenance. You have an administrative assistant who takes care of your personal appointments, lunch and dinner meetings, travel arrangements, and any other type of allocated time on your calendar. They purchase and send gifts to your loved ones and whatever else you'd like to have handled for you. Additionally, you have a couple of people who manage the financial aspects and legal requirements of all your different business interests and investments as well as your personal finances.

Those are some of the services the family office I worked at administered for family members. It was a very interesting role that provided many opportunities for me to interact with people I wouldn't have otherwise had the chance to meet. I learned different ways of thinking that helped me open my mind to new experiences.

Back in the present, I dragged my body, which felt so heavy, out of bed and walked to the bathroom. I looked at my face in the mirror, and I couldn't help but notice the dark, puffy bags under my eyes. Of course, seeing my hair strands pointing in every direction didn't help me look or feel any more put-together, but at least I knew I could conceal my dark circles and get my hair looking nice before I left the house.

"Julie," I said to myself, "how long can you keep this up? When are you going to make changes? And don't say *tomorrow* again. You know by now that tomorrow never comes."

After getting ready, I knocked a couple of times before I poked my head in my son's room. "I'm out of the bathroom and heading to work," I told him. I waited for his morning mumble to acknowledge he heard me, then continued. "You should get up now and get ready for school. Have a good day, honey."

On days like this, I had extra single-mom guilt when I left Craig to fend for himself without at least preparing breakfast for him. Craig had the responsibility of getting up and ready for school on his own since he was eight years old. He was my only child and still felt the impact of my divorce years earlier, even though his dad, Dave, and I got along reasonably well.

Dave and I had been young, in love, and—dare I say—

stupid. We got engaged after four months of dating and married by the time we'd been together for two years. We did the best we could together, but during our seventh year, when Craig was just two-and-a-half years old, we split up. Our divorce was final two months after our uncelebrated eighth anniversary.

Part of the inadequacy I felt after I divorced was that I didn't have a significant other to share the household responsibilities of bringing home the bacon and frying it up in the pan. It was up to me to do that myself, not to mention sitting down to eat the bacon before washing, drying, and putting away the pan. After that, it was Craig's homework time, and it seemed like a few seconds later it was bedtime. All those responsibilities left me stressed, overwhelmed, and depleted. Then Craig didn't always get the best of me, but his big blue eyes and cute smile always inspired me to be and do better.

On other days, I hated myself for not having the desire to date after a two-year relationship broke off, even though I wanted to get remarried. I wanted Craig to have a positive and responsible male role model in his daily life. His dad was in his life, but their time together was limited to every other weekend with sporadic phone calls between. I desperately wanted Craig to have a man to talk "guy stuff" with any time he wanted because I didn't know or understand some of those guy things. Not having a man to help support Craig in his daily home life hurt my heart, and I blamed myself for it.

At least when Craig was in elementary school, we would cuddle up under a warm, fuzzy blanket in his lower bunk bed and read Scooby-Doo from Scholastic's Book of the Month Club. Frequently, I would nod off from exhaustion while lying next to him, then jolt awake and slowly maneuver my way out of his bunk, trying not to wake him. Laundry and other chores always waited for me.

Now that he was sixteen years old, our cuddling days were long over, but my need to cram as many to-dos in as possible before practically passing out each night when I laid down in bed had gotten worse.

After I said goodbye, I headed down the stairs into the kitchen. The perpetual paper pile almost toppled off the cluttered counter as I quickly grabbed a banana for breakfast and headed down the hall. I walked down the lower set of stairs, selected the perfect pair of black pumps for my outfit from the shoe lineup on the floor mat, and opened the garage door. I had the feeling I had forgotten to do something as I unloaded all the stuff from my arms onto the passenger seat. I tried to figure out what it was. *Purse? Check. Jewelry orders? Check. Lunch bag? Check. Phone? Check. Water bottle? Check. Okay. I don't know what I'm missing, but it's time to go,* I told myself.

Dr. Wayne Dyer's *Excuses Begone* CD resumed when my car started up. I backed out of the garage and turned the volume up slightly so I could be sure to hear his every word. Listening to Dr. Dyer's words of wisdom had helped me totally retrain my brain to think abundantly a few years earlier, when I was desperately broke. Although I was now a vice president at a family office and making six figures, I continued to regularly immerse my mind in this type of purposeful programming. I called it my "university on wheels." I was sure if I kept listening, I would eventually hear the answers that would help me figure out life's meaning and my purpose in it. My life was so much easier than only a couple of years prior, when I was struggling financially, but I still felt like something was missing. I didn't know what.

As I whipped into my usual parking spot, I remembered what it was that I had forgotten to do that morning: my five-minute tapping meditation, which I had just started doing a few days earlier.

Too late now, I thought. *I'll have to do it before the tapping call with Jessica tonight.*

As I walked into work, I made a pit stop at Lisa's desk and dropped off packaged jewelry orders that had come in from clients taking advantage of the sale over the weekend. She put postage on them, added the amount I owed to my Postage Due tally sheet, and put the orders in the outgoing mail bin for me.

In addition to my job, I still had my jewelry business, but now it was on the side. Although I was no longer making jewelry because I had decided to close my business, I still had a lot of work to do. Several evenings a week, I prepared orders that I received online. Since I had a lot of items on sale, extra orders were pouring in. It helped save me time to be able to mail the orders from work instead of going to the post office every day.

I put my lunch in the refrigerator, filled up my water jug for the day, sat down at my desk, and opened my emails to check into the fire. *Did it resolve itself?* I wondered. *Or is there something I need to do?*

I scanned through the emails and saw that, although the issue was resolved, I had received additional items for my already-long to-do list. After everyone arrived, as part of my morning routine, I greeted each employee to see how they were doing and if they needed anything from me that day.

Back at my desk, I started tackling my to-do list in order of priorities. I strived for excellence in all that I did. That meant slowing down enough to think projects through, research, communicate clearly, and triple-check my work. As stewards for the family, I expected the same of my employees.

I blinked, and it was lunchtime. I made it a point to step away from my desk to eat. The break helped me clear my mind and take a breather. With my open-door policy, employees stopped by when they had questions, had an update, or needed some guidance, which often slowed my projects down. The afternoons always flew by faster than the mornings, and I never seemed to get everything completed that I wanted to. Being caught up was an impossible illusion.

More regularly than I like to admit, I'd call Craig to let him know I needed more time to finish a project and would be home late again, but I'd promise I'd be home to eat dinner together.

By the time I'd arrive home, I was often tired from working late or needed to eat quickly so I could head out the door for a spiritual workshop of some sort. If I was lucky, I had prepared a few meals ahead of time and could pop something in the microwave to warm dinner up for us. Other nights, Craig had to figure out dinner for himself.

The next day, I hit repeat. Every day was like this.

A SURPRISING SOLUTION

Around the same time, I continued to grapple with my weight. I didn't know what I was doing wrong or why I kept gaining back weight that I had lost before. I packed healthy lunches for work instead of eating out. Instead of soda pop, I drank water. And yet I kept gaining weight. On top of that, it seemed like everything I knew to eat, I could no longer eat—it made me sick. I had developed gluten and dairy intolerances and had a hard time avoiding them.

What the heck am I doing wrong? I wondered angrily. *I'm so frustrated. I don't know what the hell to eat anymore.*

Although I felt defeated and disappointed in myself for gaining back the weight, I wanted to try the whole weight loss thing again. *This time, I need to try something different,* I thought.

That's when the online course "Tapping for Weight Loss and Body Confidence" by Jessica Ortner from The Tapping Solution appeared in my life.

I had already tried EFT, or tapping, and figured it was a message from the Universe that it kept coming to my attention. A few months prior, I had looked online and found that EFT stands for Emotional Freedom Technique. Tapping is a practice of physically tapping different spots on our hands, head, face, and upper body to release emotions that are stuck in our bodies. It also helps reduce cortisol, the stress hormone. I learned that reducing cortisol helps mental chatter subside and helps us feel the better-feeling emotions. I am all for that.

I watched a few EFT videos on YouTube and was quite curious about this strange technique. I searched online, found a local community education class on EFT, and signed Kim and myself up for it. Kim and I had met several years earlier through the common loves of making beaded jewelry by hand and traveling. Over time, we also found we were both curious about healing techniques, and we got to know each other better when we traveled to attend personal growth and high-performance weekend workshops together.

In the EFT class, the instructor, Ginger, guided us to tap

along with her on each of the tapping points. She started with the location on the meatier side of the hand. Then she moved to the top of the head and down to the eyes.

"There are three tapping points around the eyes, including the inside eye up by the eyebrow, the outside corner of the eye, and under the eye on the bone," she explained. "You'll want to tap so you can feel it, but be gentle around your eyes so you don't hurt yourself."

She watched all of us to make sure we were tapping in the right places before she showed us the other two points on the face. "They are under the nose and the crease in the chin." She continued on to the collarbone and then the last point under the arm.

How am I going to remember these points? I wondered. *Am I hitting the right spot on the collarbone?*

Ginger said this is called a *tapping round.* Then we kept going, but skipped the side of the hand and instead started right back at the top of the head. There wasn't a set number of rounds each time we tapped, but she said to keep going another round or two, continuously tapping through each of the points until we felt some relief.

I thought we looked a little funny tapping on ourselves, but it didn't feel too awkward since we all were doing it together as a group. Ginger explained the points we tap on are meridian endpoints like those used in acupuncture, except we were using our fingertips instead of needles to get the energy flowing.

She continued explaining how to tap. "We tap while talking about a troublesome situation we are going through that our body feels distress about." She had us write down a difficult situation that was currently bothering us, then asked for a volunteer to demonstrate tapping in front of the group.

A lady named Sarah raised her hand and shared how upset she was with her friend Linda, who expected her to drop everything whenever she had a personal crisis in her life, which was weekly. She was tired of it and felt used because Linda never asked about her life. *Wow, she is brave,* I thought. *There is no way I am sharing my situation with the group. That's too personal.*

Then Ginger asked her how she felt inside her body and told her to rate the intensity of the sensation on a scale of zero to ten. She asked us all to do the same before we started tapping. Ginger instructed us to tap along with them as she guided Sarah to parrot out loud some of the exact things Sarah had shared with us. Sarah said she could feel sensations shifting in her body and described them while we all kept tapping. Within only a few rounds of tapping in a couple of minutes, she said, "Wow, the heavy feeling of tight air in my chest is completely gone. I'm not even upset with Linda anymore."

The strange part to me was that I also felt better, even though I didn't even tap on my own stuff. When I tapped along with them, I repeated the words Ginger said about Sarah's issue as she instructed us to do. I thought it was pretty cool that I experienced relief too! Ginger called that *borrowed benefits*. When we get clear about what we want to work on for ourselves first and then tap along with someone else's situation in the group, we all experience shifts.

Kim and I both liked how we felt at the end of class and started practicing tapping together. I also practiced on my own. The more I tapped, the more I wanted to tap, and the more I wanted to learn about it. It was very intriguing to me.

A couple of months later, I received an email about a tapping course on weight loss and body confidence. Since I was already familiar with tapping and wanted to tap more as well as lose weight, I immediately signed up for Jessica Ortner's class.

This program was different from the other weight loss programs I had done. In those programs, I had to first clear out my kitchen cupboards and refrigerator of unapproved foods and then shop for foods according to a specific food chart. Then I had to get my workout clothes ready to follow the prescribed workout routine. I always felt I had to follow it perfectly, or else I would have to start over. But this particular program didn't have any prep work, and it didn't even have a prescribed food or exercise program.

But to get us started on tapping each day, we had a guided audio meditation to tap along to that was only five minutes long.

Wait, what? I thought. *I only have to tap in the morning for five minutes on overwhelm? And the evening for five minutes on stress to get started?*

It seemed too easy.

After a few days in a row of tapping that little bit, my body felt different inside. Although I significantly shifted what I ate to remove gluten and dairy so I wouldn't have to run to the bathroom after each meal, my stomach still seemed to get upset regularly. Some form of an unsettled feeling in my gut was an uncomfortable and disconcerting new normal. But the way I felt after tapping was different. I felt calmer, and my shoulders would drop into a more relaxed position. I could breathe down through my chest and into my belly, whereas previously I wasn't able to breathe past the top of my chest. After a few minutes of tapping, I let out a massive sigh that relaxed my body. I became hopeful I could feel this way more often.

I like this calm feeling, I thought. *I want to feel this way all the time. I am going to keep tapping every morning.*

The class started a week later and was virtual, so I could do it from the comfort of my home. Each week on a ninety-minute conference call, Jessica led us through tapping by stating the tapping points and what words we should repeat. She often had a volunteer tap with her over the phone, like Ginger had in class. The rest of us tapped along with our phones on mute. Between calls, we shared our changes, emotions, and aha moments in a private Facebook group. We also had weekly videos that helped us better understand the fight-flight-freeze response, how the subconscious mind works, and the importance of working through emotions.

During one of our group conference calls, Jessica talked about how our bodies automatically go into fight-flight-freeze mode to protect us and keep us safe. She said, "When something stressful happens or you start thinking about something from your past, within seconds your brain tells your body to release adrenaline and cortisol. When that happens, it causes your digestion to slow down, which makes it harder to lose weight. It also constricts blood vessels, which negatively impacts your thinking and can increase the intensity of food cravings."

Wow, I thought. *Just by remembering something uncomfortable from my past, my body can go into fight-flight-freeze mode. Ohhhhh. I get it. That makes sense. I knew there was something more to this strange tapping thing.*

It was more than just physical relaxation that my massage therapist had noticed. While I lay bare on the massage table covered up by only a sheet, she asked me, "Are you cheating on me? Your shoulders and neck are looser."

I was surprised and quickly replied, "No, but I've been tapping." I liked the calm feeling in my belly and the loose feeling in my neck and shoulders, and I was highly motivated to keep doing it because I wanted more of those good feelings.

Before that course, I had believed I just needed to work out harder, eat healthier foods and less food in general, and use my will power and determination to lose weight. I even kept a checklist of the right behaviors and checked off the boxes each time I accomplished one of them. But during the course, I began to understand there was more to it than doing the exact right behaviors. There was a correlation between weight and emotional issues from the past. I wondered why none of the other programs I'd done had included this information. I did lose a little bit of weight during the course, but more important than that were the BIG realizations about how the brain works as well as the link between my current behavior and my past experience.

Ohhhh dang, I thought. *I probably have to deal with that crap from my childhood. Ugh. I don't know if I want to deal with it, and I don't even know how to do that. Maybe I can find an EFT practitioner near me.*

There was no way I would be able to deal with all that embarrassing childhood sexual abuse stuff on my own, and certainly not as part of the online course. It was too deep and too personal to share with a bunch of strangers online. I knew I needed to get some one-on-one help.

And frankly, I didn't want to deal with sexual abuse yet. I was too busy with my job, closing my jewelry business, and decluttering my home to prepare for an upcoming move.

Plus, I had convinced myself it wasn't that big of a deal. After all, the guy who abused me never penetrated me with his penis. So, as a result, I had put off dealing with it.

But a year later, I knew I couldn't put it off any longer. Memories began resurfacing. They started taking up too much space in my head and impacted my days. I didn't know what to do with them because every time I pushed them down, they seemed to pop back up at some inopportune time. One time at work, I was in the conference room discussing a training session with three of my employees, and it happened. We were all standing together for a quick conversation. One employee was to my left, one was standing in front of me, and the third was on my right. I felt my heart beat rapidly, my palms got sweaty, and my mouth dried up, which made it hard to speak. I wasn't in danger, but my body felt like I was under attack, like what I had experienced in the hallway at the Hurtzmans' house when I was in high school.

Chapter Two

WHACK-A-MOLE

THE HALLWAY

There were a few high school kids hanging out that day at the Hurtzmans' house. They had a sizeable, three-story home where we often congregated. We were happy to be on break from school.

Mrs. Hurtzman was in her usual position, sitting on a cushy, green fake leather high-backed stool at the breakfast bar facing into the kitchen while talking on the phone and chain-smoking cigarettes. She was 1980s multitasking at its finest.

Dan smiled at me and waved me over to follow him, like he had something secret he wanted to share with me. I followed him into the front entry hallway. There were probably five or six pairs of shoes from us kids, piled and lined up against the wall underneath the coats hanging on the hooks, which were next to the cream-colored metal door leading out to the garage.

My heart began racing. I knew something was wrong and confirmed that feeling when Dan hushed me and grabbed my wrist. *Oh fuck! Why in the world did I fall for that? I thought I was safe with all these people around. What is he going to do to me this time?*

I'd love to be able to tell you this was the first time it happened, but I don't remember the very first time. In fact, I don't remember many of the times I was abused sexually, because

31

they all blended together after a while—except for the awful ones. Those stood out as individual memories. This is one of those memories, and it was far from the first time. I knew I was about to be touched somewhere. I held back the tears.

At that moment, I found out I was the secret he wanted to share with his two football buddies, Tom Fletcher and Ben Baker. And it didn't matter that Dan hushed me, because I couldn't say anything anyway. I froze in shock and just stood there as Dan restrained me and invited his buddies to touch me wherever they wanted.

Dan was to my left. Tom was standing in front of me, with his hand reaching down my pants and then into my underwear. Ben was on my right, with his hand reaching up my shirt and underneath the elastic band on my bra, touching my breast. I couldn't believe what was happening to me. It was bad enough being groped by Dan alone, but now I was being restrained and groped by all three of them at the same time.

I had a secret crush on Tom Fletcher. I thought he was pretty cute and was hoping to catch his attention, but not in the way of what happened next. *Why is he doing this to me?* I thought. *I like him. I thought he was a nice guy. Are all guys like this?*

He began moving his fingers inside my vagina and asked, "Why is it sticky down there?"

What does he mean, "why is it sticky"? I wondered. *Oh my God. I bet I just got my period, and he's touching blood. This is so fucking embarrassing. I want to die.*

Ben quickly removed his hand from my breast and out of my bra and shirt. My heart raced even more because I got nervous that someone was coming, since his actions were so abrupt. Then he said, "We need to stop this. This isn't right."

Thank God, I prayed.

Tom's hand came out of my underwear and pants. The firm restraint around my wrists released, and I took a deep breath in as the four of us slowly turned and walked out of the hallway. They went into the living room area like nothing had happened, and I went to the bathroom to gather myself and straighten out my undergarments. I confirmed that I did have my period. Tom's fingers had been touching my blood.

That is so gross, I thought.

I could feel my face getting warm. My cheeks turned red from the combination of embarrassment about my period and feeling stupid and angry with myself for falling for Dan's plan. I wanted to stay in the bathroom forever so I wouldn't have to see any of them again. But another small part of me still hoped Tom would ask me out.

I joined the group in the living room. I sat down next to Dan's sister and acted as if everything was normal. Although I vividly recall the details of the hallway groping and going into the bathroom, I have no idea what happened after that. But I do know that the four of us from the hallway never talked about it. I never told anyone, Tom Fletcher never asked me out, and Dan continued to abuse me.

EMOTIONAL FREEDOM TECHNIQUE

Other memories like that periodically resurfaced. It felt like I was living that stupid whack-a-mole game, where a memory would pop up through a hole, I would whack it down, and another one would pop up through a different hole. I sought out an EFT practitioner near me to see if I could get some help, because I was tired of playing that emotional pop-up game.

I looked online, found a couple of practitioners in my area, and saw that one of them taught EFT certification classes for EFT Universe, an organization that trains and certifies people to help others by using this technique. I love to learn, and I decided to sign up for a Level 1 EFT certification class, but not with the intention that I would become an EFT practitioner.

This stuff works amazingly well, I thought. *It brings up so many emotions from my memories, and I feel better afterward. But I don't want to be a practitioner because it looks a little weird to tap on my body and talk out loud about my thoughts and memories. I just want to learn how to use this more effectively for myself.*

In the class, I met another student, Bobby, who I felt instantly connected with for some reason. During a short morning break, we stayed seated and turned our chairs to face each other. My body leaned forward, listening intently as she shared how the integrative health coaching program she was finishing taught her that food isn't the cause of weight gain.

"Not effectively dealing with our emotions from our past causes it," she said, which was what led her to the EFT class. "It's an effective tool I can use with my clients to help them deal with their emotions, which will ultimately help them lose weight."

I shared that I had learned the same information in the online tapping course I took with Jessica Ortner from The Tapping Solution. "During class, memories resurfaced from childhood sexual abuse," I blurted out, surprising myself. I didn't usually share such personal information like that with strangers.

The instructor, Rita, said it was time for class to resume.

We moved our chairs back, facing forward. Bobby leaned in and whispered, "Me too. I will share more at lunch."

Chills tingled in my arms, and I smiled, thinking how lucky I was to sit next to her. On a piece of my notebook paper, I wrote, *I don't know how to explain it, but I feel really connected to you.* I slowly tore it out of my notebook so I wouldn't disrupt anyone with the paper rustling noise. I slid it on the table over to her.

She wrote something and pushed it back to me. *Same here.*

I looked at her. We silently exchanged smiles, and I felt my heart smile too. I wasn't alone.

At lunch, we found two seats away from the group, where we could quietly finish our deeply personal conversation. She leaned in and spoke just above a whisper. "Julie, I don't know how to explain this, but I felt compelled to reach out to the person who hurt me." She paused for a moment. "It was my uncle. I wanted to have a conversation with him. I wasn't interested in yelling at him, prosecuting him, or anything like that. I just felt strongly that I needed to talk to him after having several therapy sessions."

Wow, I thought. *She is brave for having reached out like that.*

I couldn't imagine reaching out to the person who abused me to have a conversation with him. At the time, I didn't fully understand why she needed to do that. But she told me it had helped her, her uncle, and his wife a lot. She was pleased that she did it despite others encouraging her not to open the can of worms from the past.

The next day, I arrived after Bobby, and someone was already sitting next to her. So I sat toward the back of the room next to Patti. We were both pretty quiet students, but when we talked on break, we discovered that neither of us had intended to get certified as practitioners when we signed up for class. Now, after our experience in class, we both were leaning toward getting certified. We exchanged contact information and agreed we would get in touch to tap together to help each other with certification requirements. Little did we know that five years later, we'd both still be tapping together!

Still inspired by Bobby's story at the end of the two-day workshop, I felt like it was time for me to take another step to get some help with healing my past. After class, I set up a one-on-one tapping appointment with Rita.

At age forty-three, I had only shared with a small handful of people that I had experienced sexual abuse, and I was too ashamed and embarrassed to talk about it in any detail. I arrived a few minutes early for my appointment after work. She shared an office with a chiropractor and called me into the room. She invited me to sit down in the chair while she closed the door behind me. Even though I wanted to do this, my palms were sweaty, and my insides were tightened up. I looked around, trying to figure out if the walls were solid enough that no one would be able to hear me. I couldn't tell if they were or not and didn't get a chance to inquire because she interrupted my thoughts, asking, "What would you like to focus on, Julie?"

Reluctantly I said, "I want to work on the sexual abuse memories. But I don't know where to start, and I don't want to speak the memories out loud." My shoulders tensed up. It was humiliating for me, and I felt a lot of shame about the whole situation. She suggested we start slow and easy by saying my abuser's name out loud while tapping. Although it sounded simple enough to say his name, I immediately got a big lump in the back of my throat, and I could feel the tears forming behind my eyes. I was so emotionally choked up that I could hardly speak. I didn't want to say his name out loud, but I followed her lead and started tapping on the top of my head too.

"Julie, what is his first name?"

I was silent. His name wouldn't come out of my mouth. She shifted to the next tapping point by the eyebrow, and I followed. We tapped in silence for a few moments before I could mutter, "Dan."

Instantly the pooled tears overflowed and splashed down my cheeks. But Rita directed me to keep tapping. It was hard to tap because I was crying so hard. Sobbing, really.

"Julie, you have to keep tapping no matter what. This is really important," she said.

I felt so embarrassed about crying so hard about a person's name that I couldn't even look at her. But out of my peripheral view, I saw Rita nod her head encouragingly and say, "You're doing well, Julie. When you're able to speak again, repeat his name while continuing to tap."

I wish I would have told that one therapist this stuff when I was fifteen, I thought. *My parents forced me to see her because I was so angry. If I had said something back then, I wouldn't have had to go through all of this now. But I never said a word. Damn it!*

Back then, my brother Joe and I had both been called down to the main office at Mounds View High School. I was a freshman, and he was a sophomore. The lady in the office had told us our dad would be there to pick us up and to wait by the door. I immediately thought something had happened to Grandpa K. because he had been sick. My dad never picked me up at school in the middle of the day before without telling me in advance. His silver Toyota Camry pulled into the circle drive, and he stopped at the front door. Joe hopped in the front seat, and I sat in the back. Almost simultaneously we asked, "Is Grandpa okay?"

Dad responded, "Yes, he is. That's not what this is about. We are going to a therapy appointment, and your mom is meeting us there."

Whoa. This is a big deal if Mom is meeting us there, I thought. *She never takes off work in the middle of the day.*

My parents had divorced when I was six or seven. They got along pretty well, and apparently well enough to go to this appointment together. I wasn't excited about this at all. In fact, I felt a knot in the pit of my stomach, but at least we were all going together.

When we all were seated in the therapist's office, I was shocked to find out *I* was the reason we were there. I don't remember who said I was angry all the time. But after I heard that, everything went into slow motion. All the mental chatter stopped except for the plotting my brain was doing to plan my escape.

I don't recall how far into the appointment we were when I decided it was time to get up and make a run for it. I opened the door and ran down the hall, down the stairs, and out the main entrance of the building. My dad was behind me, but I had run in track sixth, seventh, and eighth grade, so I thought I could outrun him. I was wise enough to look both ways before I darted across the busy street into a wooded area where my dad caught up with me. I had forgotten he was a runner too. I don't remember what he said to me, but I do remember between my heart racing and tears streaming down my face that I could hardly breathe. My dad made me go back to that room. I felt so defeated. I shuffled back as slowly as possible, with my head facing the ground so I wouldn't have to look at anyone.

"Julie, I am glad you came back to join us. You can sit in that chair away from the door," said the way-too-happy-sounding therapist. I plopped down in the chair, crossed my arms, and stared at the floor. After that dreadful session, I had to go back and do therapy sessions by myself.

I don't remember how many sessions I went to or what we talked about, but three other sessions stick out in my mind. During one of those sessions, the therapist asked me if anyone was hurting me. "No," I lied. I was afraid that if I said yes, I would get in trouble. They would think I'd done something wrong and that it was my fault for letting him touch me.

During another session I recall, I had to take a personality test. While I was taking the test, my body was tense with worry. *Will she be able to tell by my answers that Dan is touching me?* I wondered. *What if they find out I am not a virgin?*

The next week, during the last session I remember, the therapist shared the results with me and my dad. She sounded surprised that I was a well-adapted teen with a little anger. I tried not to show my relief that they hadn't found out my secrets. Now, all these years later, I wish they had figured it out. I wish I had told them. It's easy to say that in hindsight, knowing if I had dealt with it right away, it could have stopped and wouldn't have caused all these other issues in my life. And I wouldn't have to sit in an office in my forties, tapping on my face and saying his name.

It seemed like a long time before I could speak, but it was probably one or two minutes. Still tapping, I repeated his name.

"Dan. Dan. Dan. Dan. Dan."

I glanced up at her with my head still pointed down. Her eyelids were drooped, and her lower lip protruded downward as if she felt my pain and sorrow too. I could feel the compassion radiating from her, and she assured me I would feel relief soon. Still feeling ashamed, I quickly looked back down.

I couldn't believe that, more than twenty-five years since the very last time he pinned me to the floor and inserted his fingers and tongue up my vagina, just saying his name would make me break down and cry. I was amazed at the powerlessness I felt by speaking out loud a three-letter name, especially since he never put his penis inside of me. I wanted those gross feelings gone. I kept tapping while repeating his name over and over.

"Dan. Dan. Dan. Dan."

For years, I had been felt up, held down, hushed, and threatened by my neighbor. He was my brother's friend and my friend's brother. The four of us hung out regularly. He forcefully touched me in places I had neither been touched nor wanted to be touched. We were supposed to be friendly neighbors, but not like that.

It had started when I was eleven. Six years later, when I was seventeen, it finally ended.

I vividly remember the day it ended and about three others. They are ingrained in my brain like an etching in stone because I was surprise-attacked, repeatedly held against my will, and forcefully touched. But the truth is, the abuse only physically stopped at age seventeen. In reality, the abuse continued in my mind and body for years and years. Just the thought of any one of those days caused a firehose of adrenaline to flood through my body and put me on edge. Traumatic scenes periodically replayed over and over in my head. The feelings of shame, guilt, and embarrassment surged over and over through my body.

I don't know how long I tapped, but I kept tapping until

my throat cleared, my body felt relief inside, and the tears stopped streaming. I started feeling better, and it got easier and more comfortable to say his name. My body let out a huge sigh, and I felt the cells in my stomach calm. His name was now just a name I could easily say.

The impact of tapping on just his name was profound. I realized that stuffing down the memories from the past, ignoring them, and pretending they didn't exist no longer worked for me. And if I was entirely honest with myself, those methods never worked. They led to other behaviors like stuffing my face with ice cream to numb the pain, which led to feelings of guilt and ultimately increased weight. Then that led to a vicious roller-coaster cycle of working hard to lose weight only to gain it back and then some.

I wanted to dig deep to get these feelings out, and this seemed to be the right solution. And I clearly had more work to do, because as I tapped on one memory, others resurfaced. It was like I was pulling a thread from a spool and trying to find the end, but it was buried deep in the center. I would have to keep pulling the thread to get there.

I continued to meet with Rita for six sessions. Although I felt massive relief after each tapping session with her, I knew that there was a lot more to dig into. I didn't have a clue about what was involved with healing from my past. I believed that working with a therapist who specialized in trauma and abuse was in my best interest. If I was going to dig in deep to do the work, I wanted to find someone with experience in that area who could help me work through all the aspects of my sexual abuse. I pulled up a website to start searching for a therapist who could help me.

Chapter Three
DIGGING DEEP

TAKING THE DIVE

A few weeks after my last tapping session, I remembered that Bobby from the EFT certification class a few months earlier had told me about her therapist. I reached out to Bobby on Facebook Messenger, and she provided me with her therapist's name—Penny—and gave her a glowing recommendation.

However, when I called to make an appointment with Penny, her schedule was filled. The next available opening for a new client was six weeks out. *Ah man! This fricking sucks*, I thought. *I am finally ready, and now I have to wait. But she's probably excellent if she has a wait-list. I've waited this long. I can wait a little longer.*

The day of my first appointment arrived. I checked in at the reception desk and took a seat. I distracted myself from my worry by looking around at the other people waiting for their appointments. I wondered what issues all these people were coming here to get a handle on. Were they the same as mine, or something else?

Just then, Penny poked her head out from behind the brown wooden office door into the waiting room where I was sitting. "Julie?" She smiled.

I got up, we greeted each other with a nod and "Hello," and I smiled back. "It's nice to meet you," we said at the same time.

She gestured with her open arm and fingers pointing down the hall. "My office is this way."

I followed her. Although she came highly recommended by Bobby, I looked her over, sizing her up to determine if she was going to be a good therapist for me, as if somehow I could tell by the way she looked. Nonetheless, I was pleased. She seemed nice already with her warm smile, pleasant voice, and welcoming manners. Plus, I trusted Bobby, who said she was an excellent guide and could do amazing things to help me.

She invited me into her office. I glanced around to familiarize myself with the layout of her spacious yet cozy-feeling office. It was decorated like a living room, with comfy furniture, green plants, and a beautiful picture of a sunset on the wall. She sat down in a tall, padded black office chair with her back to the windows and invited me to sit down on an overstuffed dark-brown leather couch facing her. I picked up the cushy burgundy couch pillow and clutched it in front of me, unknowingly for protection and comfort.

I hope she is an excellent guide for me too, I thought. *I am tired of struggling. I'm ready for my life to shift for the better! It's time!*

But we didn't dive in right away. Penny let me know that our first appointment would be spent filling out intake forms and asking questions so she could get to know me. It took most of the hour to complete the required (and over-the-top, in my opinion) stack of paperwork. After I answered the somewhat invasive personal questions, I threw out a couple of additional answers for her. "My shoe size is eight, and you can't have my firstborn."

Penny chuckled and told me she thought we were going to have a good time together with my sense of humor.

I felt like I could trust her already. *She genuinely laughs at my jokes and is so kind. I think this is going to work out just fine with her.*

But now that the paperwork was over, I felt nervous. I took a deep breath and explained why I had come here. I let Penny know I was abused sexually between ages eleven and seventeen. I was there, in her office, because I wanted the awful memories of being held down and touched against my will to stop flashing through my head. Memories seemed to be popping up more frequently since I had tapped on his name. It was as if they were trying to get my attention so I would address them too. I asked her if she'd be able to help me so I could stop feeling like I was going crazy.

She assured me that's exactly what she would help me with and told me it was vital for me to know this journey would be emotional, and I'd need to make time for lots of self-care and fun activities to support my healing.

Well, I am already good at self-care, I thought. *I get massages to get the knots out of my shoulders and relax my body. Plus, I go to the chiropractor to help my body realign, so that should be good. I always feel lighter afterward, so I will keep doing that.*

I nodded in agreement and then asked Penny to tell me about EMDR. I knew it stood for "eye movement something something" and that it was similar to EFT. Penny explained it stood for *eye movement desensitization and reprocessing*, and it would help my brain process the emotions from the memories that stuck from when the traumas occurred. She said some therapists moved a lighted wand back and forth in front of their client's face and have the client follow the light with their eyes. But she used a handy little TENS machine because it seemed to work better, and I wouldn't have the light in my eyes or even have to move my eyes back and forth.

"What's a TENS machine?" I asked. She told me that TENS stands for *transcutaneous electrical nerve stimulation.*

"Trans cue something . . . Hopefully, there won't be a test later," I said, laughing nervously.

She chuckled, confirmed there wouldn't be a test, and continued to explain how it worked. She held up a white control box in one hand and two small black paddles in the other. I could see that the paddles connected to wires that attached to the control box. She handed me the paddles and instructed me to put one in each hand. I folded my fingers over my palms to lightly grip onto the paddles. She turned the box on so I could feel an electrical pulse alternating between my left and right hands. Then she explained she would have me focus on a specific memory as well as the emotions and sensations that I felt in my body.

"So, essentially, you'll be zapping the emotions and feelings of the memories out of my head?" I inquired.

She chuckled and said it would be something like that. She suggested I think of the trauma like a splinter in a finger. It's uncomfortable to have a small piece of wood or glass stuck in your finger. Your body needs help to get it unstuck and out of your skin. If you don't remove it, it could fester and become more painful and even infected. But once you remove the splinter, then the pain will go away and your body can heal the injury. She said we would be working together to remove the traumatic splinters from my past.

I looked at Penny with that reluctant *Fine, let's do this, but I don't want to* expression on my face. You know the one I'm talking about: the one that goes with a little temper tantrum in your mind because you know you need to deal with the situation and will feel better afterward, but you also dread it because you know the "doing" part of it sucks rocks. Yeah, that look. I'm sure she had seen that look many times before, from other people who wanted the haunting memories out of their heads too.

Man, I'm nervous about how I'm going to feel when I share all this, I thought. *I don't want to break down and cry. I just want to feel sane again. I hope this works.*

Before I knew it, our session was over. I was a little disappointed we didn't have time to try the zapper on a memory so I could see if it worked, but we had the opportunity to use it several times over the next few months. The zapper itself was pain-free, but the emotions and memories that came up weren't.

LOOKING OVER MY SHOULDER

In our second session, as I sat in that overstuffed leather couch again, Penny guided me to close my eyes and find the happy place in my mind where I could go to relax, which for me was the beach. I was born and raised in Minnesota in the cold Midwest, but when I could afford to take trips, I usually chose a warm destination with the beach nearby. I love the sand in my toes, the sun shining down from the blue sky warming my skin, and the sound of the ocean waves crashing on the beach with a little breeze moving through the palm trees. That's my happy place and has been since I was in elementary school. In the cold Minnesota winter, when I stood outside waiting for the heated school bus to hurry and pick me up, I imagined I was in Hawaii in the warm sunshine. It worked for me to pretend back then. Hopefully, it would work now too.

Penny explained the benefit of finding that place in my mind to retreat so that my mind and body could start to relax. "Julie," she said, guiding me with her soothing voice, "let go and relax your body."

I imagined myself on the beach and tried to relax into the soft white sand, but I just couldn't. Even though I knew I was in a safe place, I didn't feel safe. I had a strange feeling inside, like I had to look over my shoulder. I burst into tears.

"Oh my God," I cried. "I don't even know how to relax."

Penny responded calmly and told me my body was doing its job to protect me. She said I didn't need to worry, because we would keep working on it so my body could fully relax.

It wasn't actually that I didn't know how to relax. It was that my body literally couldn't relax because it was vigilantly protecting me. It had been protecting me twenty-four hours a day, seven days a week, 365 days a year since I was a kid. It was trying to keep me safe from a possible impending attack.

Learning of my inability to relax helped me understand on a deeper level the fight-flight-freeze mode I had learned about in Jessica Ortner's class and even more in the EFT certification class. Fight-flight-freeze (aka the stress response) occurs when you face something scary and your body reacts to protect you. First, a surge of hormones is released, your heartbeat increases, and you breathe faster. Plus, blood flows to the major muscle groups so you can strike out or run away. At the same time, blood flows away from the digestive and other systems so your body can put all its resources into protecting you. Your food will need to get digested later.

This can result in behavioral responses that you don't understand. For example, you might yell at your partner for embarrassing you in front of your friends (fight). Or you might feel uncomfortable with all the people at a party, so you leave early (flight). Or your mind might go blank when you're standing up, speaking in front of a group of people (freeze). All these scenarios can cause anxiety, which can trigger the stress response in your body. It becomes tense and ready for action to protect you from danger—real or perceived—so that you can survive.

For me, when I was surprise-attacked or held against my will in my childhood, my body went into the stress response. I never knew which response it would go into: fight, flight, or freeze. I had experienced all of them during different attacks. But because I experienced trauma so many times in my childhood, my body continued to operate in that stress response regularly, even during perceived threats. Being in this state for years and years harmed my body. So if my body was always on high alert and trying to stay safe, then other systems in my body weren't able to function properly unless they became severe, creating an emergency for my body to attend to them.

At the beginning of the next three sessions, Penny continued to guide me to find a happy place in my mind to help my body calm down and get out of protection mode. She wanted me to figure out my happy place for myself, instead of telling me what to visualize. I stuck with the beach scene, imagining I was in one of those overwater bungalows in Bora Bora like I had seen in a travel magazine photo. The bungalow had a thatched roof, and I visualized the beautiful blue ocean water beneath my feet through the glass floor panel.

"Julie, do you see yourself in your happy place?" Penny asked.

My body shifted side to side on the couch, trying to feel relaxed. I smiled as I told her I could see myself there and even saw a tiny, colorful fish swimming under my feet and some dolphins swimming and jumping over in the distance off to my left. They looked like they were having fun, and they made me smile.

She gave me an attagirl and guided me to lie back in the hammock to try to relax again. I heard Penny say the word "relax," but I felt my body sitting up straight on her couch with my right hand bracing the armrest. So this time, when I saw myself plopping down in a hammock, just as I sat back, I noticed I quickly looked over my shoulder to see if anyone was coming. Then I felt intense sadness inside my heart for the part of me that always felt like I had to be on the lookout for something terrible.

Then, all of a sudden, I felt my chest tighten up. My heart beat faster as I told Penny what I had just experienced and that I didn't want to lie back because I didn't feel safe yet.

She suggested I have someone there with me to help keep a watch out and protect me so I could fully relax. "Have them stand away from you so you have your own space to relax. Where would you like them to stand?" she asked.

I didn't even consciously know who I was on the lookout for other than any male who could hurt me. But with my eyes still closed, I took a deep breath in and imagined the security guard standing over on the white sandy beach while I was in the bungalow, taking my flip-flops off my feet. I lowered my body back into the hammock. I took another deep breath in and slowly let it out. I felt my body sink into the couch.

Knowing the security guard was on the beach helped me to relax for the first time in who the hell knows how long.

"How are you doing, Julie?" Penny asked. "Can you feel your body relaxing?"

I told her I was in the hammock, actually relaxing. It wasn't exactly what I would call comfortably relaxing. But I was in the hammock, and I could see the beautiful blue sky, puffy white clouds, and dolphins jumping out of the water off in the distance again. She applauded me for my progress and told me I'd need to keep practicing relaxation between our sessions, with the goal of relaxing in my happy place without the security guard on the beach protecting me.

I kept practicing, and eventually I was able to comfortably relax without the guard—or anyone else, for that matter. The first time that happened, I let out a huge sigh, and happy tears streamed down my cheeks. I was so relieved to know I was making progress, calming my mind and body. Plus, I was proud of my progress and excited to tell Penny that I was able to relax without anyone having to stand there to protect me.

After she congratulated me, she told me the next step to take when at home was to go to that space daily. "You'll need to sit on your couch and do nothing. Just be. Then go to that happy space to let your mind know you're safe."

I knew the more I practiced, the easier it would be, and the better I'd feel. But I didn't understand what she meant by "sit on the couch and do nothing."

WTF? How can I do that? I have a gazillion other things to do. I can't just sit around.

Confused, I asked, "So you're saying to just sit on a couch or a chair . . . and just be?"

She nodded, confirming my understanding.

"Seriously, Penny?" I asked hesitantly. "That's boring, and I don't have time for that."

Penny shook her head, leaned forward toward me, and said, "Julie, you're going to need to make time for it. Your subconscious mind has been in fight-flight-freeze mode, working on overdrive to keep you safe since you were a young child. As we continue to work together, you're going to need to listen to your body and give it what it needs to heal. That may mean taking a walk in the park, napping on the couch, journaling your feelings, soaking in a warm bubble bath, or just sitting and relaxing. It's your job to support your body and give it whatever it needs."

I stared off into space for a moment, pondering the thought of just sitting. I didn't like the idea at all. It sounded lazy to me, and I didn't want to become a lazy person. I didn't like lazy people. She must have seen a look on my face because she asked me what was going on in my mind and if I had a concern about something.

I told her I was honestly afraid just to sit to relax. I had always been an extremely productive person. I had accomplished a lot in life and was worried I would be too lazy and wouldn't get anything done if I relaxed while just sitting. I prided myself on getting stuff done. In fact, I was lovingly called an overachiever by many of my friends.

I recalled a time I was on the phone with a friend while cleaning up the kitchen and sharing the various projects I was working on. He asked me, "Do you ever just relax, Julie?" I didn't understand why he would ask me such a ridiculous question. I told him I could relax, but I didn't have time for that. I had things I wanted to accomplish in my life, and I couldn't achieve them by being lazy and sitting on my ass.

After all, life is short, and I don't want to have any regrets that I didn't accomplish things on my bucket list.

The only time I would relax was when I was sick in bed. Even then, that was only out of necessity because my body had shut down with pneumonia or migraine headaches. And it wasn't very relaxed, because I'd impatiently wait for my body to hurry up and heal. I was like a child taking a long car ride, asking every fifteen minutes, "Are we there yet?"

When I was sick, I wouldn't have the energy to do much more than sleep. Sometimes my head would hurt so much that I couldn't make my way out of bed and would stay there for hours or days with a pillow covering my eyes. I hated the times I got sick because it felt like such a waste of time and a waste of my paid time off from work. Not to mention I felt like a shitty single mom when my son had to fend for himself even more because I was in bed. It seemed like the frequency of being sick had increased in the past couple of years.

"Julie, are you able to commit to self-care?" Penny asked.

I felt my face scrunch up in reluctance as I thought, *I know Penny has had life experiences that I haven't. She's helped other people heal. She probably knows what she's talking about. I better do it.*

My chest and shoulders lifted up and then dropped back down as I let out a sigh. "Fine, Penny! I will try relaxing. Even though I don't want to!" I said with an exaggerated resistant attitude and a smile.

Through therapy, I learned that I had developed that super-productive overachiever trait as a protective measure. That was another way my subconscious mind protected me and kept me safe. In addition to working full-time, if I kept busy with projects, taking more classes, selling off the remaining inventory of my handmade jewelry, and decluttering my home, then I wouldn't have to think about or deal with my past.

Being an overachiever had become part of my identity. My friends, family, boss, and coworkers all knew if I committed to something, I would get it done on time and with excellence no matter what. They could always count on me, and I was proud of that. It was like an overachiever badge of honor I proudly carried on me at all times.

I then made the connection that the reason I had been getting so sick recently was because I was overworking myself. My subconscious, in trying to protect me from harm, pushed me to work harder than I needed to. And at the same time, my body had been on high alert, always ready for potential danger. I began to understand how my past trauma was still controlling my life.

Chapter Four

DIGGING IN DEEPER

SABBATICAL

After my seventh or eighth session with Penny, she announced she'd be moving in a couple of months. "Julie, I feel I need to let you know that I am moving to another office. July thirty-first is my last day here."

My heart sank, and I'm sure my mouth dropped open. "Fuck," I said out loud. "Oh no. You can't move. We just got started," I added in a panicky voice.

With her head slightly tilted to the left, Penny looked at me in a soft, *I-am-sorry* gaze. "I know. I feel bad, Julie. I like working with you, and we are making some nice progress, but that's why I wanted to tell you right away. I can help you find another therapist if you don't want to continue with me, knowing I will be moving."

Another therapist was the last thing I wanted. After all that time of putting off dealing with my crap, I was finally open to working through it and looked forward to going to therapy because of Penny. I liked and trusted her and wanted to keep working with her.

"Where are you moving to, Penny? Can I drive there for appointments?" I asked, feeling desperate yet determined.

"Well, it's a bit far, Julie. It's a good hour and a half away. I am moving to be closer to my dad, who has some health concerns."

"Oh, I see. Well, that's nice. You'll get to be closer to your dad."

Damn it! I don't want to start this process over and find a new therapist. Maybe I can double up on my appointments. Will insurance cover that for me? I wondered.

After our session, I called my insurance company to find out how often under their plan I could see Penny. I was pleased with their response that I could see her as many times as I needed, just not more than once a day. Over the next few weeks, I did the exact opposite of what all of her other clients were doing. Instead of tapering off sessions with her and transitioning to a new therapist, I doubled up on my appointments and saw her twice a week in June.

During the first few therapy sessions, the initial relief I felt at the end of each session didn't last long. Surprisingly, inside I felt like a train getting derailed off the tracks while still picking up speed. I thought I should be feeling better, not worse. In hindsight, I know it was all the dust and dirt stirring up from the internal house cleaning that had been going on. Anyone who has gone through therapy knows it gets messier before it gets clean when you're healing from deep trauma.

Oh my God, what is happening to me? I can't even think clearly or stay focused on anything, I thought. *Is this what it feels like to have a nervous breakdown? I need a break from my life.*

Work was tough for me. I had been the vice president at a family office for the past five years. I prided myself on being a stellar, overachieving employee, but all of a sudden I found myself distracted. I struggled with managing my employees and focusing on all my projects. In my mind, I felt like a discombobulated mess. I felt like I was failing even though

I probably didn't look like it on the outside because I was still getting work done and meeting all my deadlines.

What am I going to do? How do I fix this?

During this time, I learned that one of the partners at the accounting firm we used was going on a three-month, company-paid sabbatical. *Now there's an idea,* I thought. *Maybe I can take a sabbatical.*

I had never thought of taking a sabbatical before. I didn't even know precisely what a sabbatical looked like other than from the movies. I thought of scenes of people going off to India for a month-long silent retreat. I wasn't prepared to do that, but I didn't know what else I would do with the time off. I just felt like I desperately needed time and space to clear my head and figure out a plan. Even though I designated my remaining earned vacation time for an upcoming financial coaching certification program, I decided to have a conversation with my boss about this sabbatical idea.

I realize that's not a typical conversation an employee has with their boss because, first of all, not all employees are eligible for a sabbatical if their company even offers it. And secondly, most US companies aren't in the mindset of paying for additional time off for workers. In fact, in the US, a lot of employers still look at their employees as liabilities rather than assets. They try to get as much work out of them as possible. They may not want to or not be able to pay them to take additional time off above and beyond the minimal vacation pay allotted. At the family office, we didn't have a sabbatical policy. I'd never even thought of asking for a full month off before. I'd only dreamed of it in the past, imagining I would travel to Europe or take a month-long cruise. I didn't believe I could afford to do it.

But Doug and I had developed a mutual respect and admiration for each other over the six years we'd worked together. I had worked hard for him and earned his trust by serving him and his family well; in return, he had invested in my personal growth. I'd never experienced that type of relationship with a boss before and knew it didn't come along every day.

We walked outside across the parking lot and sat down on the bench at the wooden picnic table, underneath a pergola with grapevines hanging down. The vines expanded across the beams, creating a cool sunshade. Despite feeling a little nervous inside, I started the conversation and let my boss, Doug Burrman, know I was struggling personally and didn't know how to explain it very well. I shared that I'd had scenes popping into my mind from childhood trauma, and they were making it hard for me to focus on anything else. I told him I had allotted my remaining paid time off for my trip in July, but I wanted to know if I could take the month of July off, like a sabbatical. But I'd take it unpaid.

Sounding surprised, Doug clarified, "The whole month of July off?"

I nodded, confirming that was what I had requested.

He immediately responded, "No."

I felt my breath stop.

He continued, "A month is too long. I need you here to manage the employees to keep things going."

I was taken aback because, in my hurry to find relief, I hadn't thought through how I would respond to the possibility of Doug saying no. I felt desperate inside and knew I needed time off, even though I didn't know what I was going to do with it. I let out a big sigh, and before I realized what I was saying, the words just fell out of my mouth. "May I work part-time in July?"

He glanced over at me and paused for a moment before he responded with a confirming nod. "That may work, as long as you have set hours. You'll need to set up a schedule for yourself."

I told him I could do that and would get back to him with an exact plan. Without hesitation, he replied, "I will pay you full time. I know you've been working hard on building your emergency fund. You don't need to use that up."

Tears welled up behind my eyes. I felt immense gratitude swell in my heart for my boss, who was honoring my request and so much more than I had ever asked for, imagined, or expected. "Wow. Thank you, Doug. Thank you so much. I really appreciate your generosity." I paused to hold back the tears so they wouldn't come out of my eyes and stream down my face. "Thank you. I accept. I could work from nine a.m. until one p.m. each day."

He replied that that would work fine and then said, "It is an honor for me that I get to support people who are doing their personal work."

We exchanged heartfelt smiles, then got up off the wooden bench and headed across the parking lot back into the building.

FULLY COMMITTING TO SELF-CARE

At my next session with Penny, I told her about my schedule for July and asked if I could handle seeing her every day. I wasn't wondering if I would get sick of working with her, but rather if my mind could handle that much therapy. Then I joked she might get sick of me.

Penny looked me squarely in the eyes and firmly told me that I could only do it if I got serious about self-care. This meant self-care every single day and not just massage and chiropractic. She had previously suggested going on walks, taking baths, just sitting and being, and even taking naps if my body needed it, but I hadn't consistently done any of them. It was clear from her firm, direct tone that it was no longer a suggestion, but rather a requirement. I would need to take it seriously and honor my body during this process.

Nothing like moving full speed ahead and immersing myself, I thought as I shook my head with an eye roll and a snicker. *I do it in other areas of my life. I might as well do it with healing work too.*

I agreed I would fully take care of myself and scheduled as many therapy sessions as their system allowed. Luckily, compared to the six-week wait a couple of months ago, it was now a lot easier to find open times on her schedule almost every day, because her other clients were winding down their time with her.

At first, it was a little awkward figuring out how to add self-care to my life. I already had so much going on that adding in doing nothing felt like a chore. I looked at my calendar to see where the open time slots were and then contacted my walking buddy, Diane, to set up a weekly self-care walking date. That was the first significant step. It was healing for me to share with her some of the things I worked on in therapy because it helped me understand things even better when I explained them to someone else. And for her, she appreciated my openness and vulnerability, which helped her in her life too. In return, she opened up and shared her stories with me. We both felt light and free afterward.

In another self-care attempt, I filled up the bathtub and sat in at as long as I could tolerate it, which was probably ten minutes at the most. I didn't relax because I was scrolling on my cell phone, checking email and Facebook. Yes, while in the bathtub. I struggled doing nothing while just sitting there, but I realized how ridiculous I was being by not setting my phone down. So I promised myself that next time I would leave my cell phone out of reach.

In July, I worked the 9:00 a.m. to 1:00 p.m. schedule Doug and I had talked about, went to therapy after work, and then practiced self-care. Penny was right: The intensity of therapy pushed me to take a crash course in extreme self-care to honor my mind and body. That month, I learned how to just sit without reading or doing paperwork or anything else. I learned to leave the to-do lists for some other day. I learned to nap after therapy if I was tired instead of thinking I was a wimp if I didn't push through until my designated bedtime. And I used my cell phone to play meditation music when I took baths. Slowly my mental chatter quieted, and my body continued to calm down.

After many of our sessions, I journaled about how I felt about the memories that crept into my mind. I was determined to clear them out one way or another. At that point, the pain of clearing out all the emotions that I felt was way better than the pain of leaving them in, so I figured I might as well press on. I found it was quite healing, putting pen to paper and writing about what was going on in my mind as well as noticing the sensations I felt in my body. I also added tapping to the mix to help me release the emotions after journaling. That always calmed the inside of my body, even when it didn't initially feel stressed or upset.

When Diane wasn't available, I started to enjoy taking walks by myself just for the sake of moving my body and connecting with nature. Every walk I had taken before this always had an agenda behind it: to burn calories on a mission to lose weight. Walking to walk and clear my mind felt great and took the pressure to achieve something off me. On these walks, I took the time to notice the different kinds of trees and appreciate the shapes of their leaves and the shade they provided along the black, tar-paved walking trail. I spent time enjoying the bright orangish-yellow black-eyed Susans in the field, a white heron on the lakeshore, and even a cute little gray bunny that let me take some close-up photos before he hopped off the walking path into the woods.

The next day, I proudly told Penny, "I napped yesterday after our session. When I woke, I even sat on the deck. I watched the birds and squirrels scurrying for seeds that had fallen from the bird feeder hanging off my neighbors' deck."

Her eyes twinkled like a proud momma watching her child walk for the first time, and she told me I had come a long way since we first started together just a couple of months earlier. I thanked her and laughed at what I was about to tell her. "I am surprisingly pleased with my accomplishment of doing nothing. Ironically, I feel deeply satisfied. I don't think I'd ever received kudos for doing nothing, Penny. But it feels good to slow down and take care of myself."

And for the first time, I began to listen to my body consistently. I got quiet, asked what it needed, and patiently listened in silence. I heard different messages. At first, I thought I was making shit up. But the more I slowed down and paid attention in silence, the more I could hear my body quietly asking for what it needed. I think my crazy mental chatter was so loud before that it drowned out that quiet, wise, intuitive voice.

The craziest thing happened too. When I slowed down and took the time to listen, I got more accomplished, and sometimes it felt like I was somehow magically getting things done without doing anything—even just the little things. For example, on my to-do list I had listed to call a specific person, but I just sat there for a moment, thinking about calling them. Within the next day or so, they called me. I didn't have to do anything other than answer the phone when they called. That hadn't been the norm before. I often played phone tag with people. But now it was kind of spooky-cool how they called me at the perfect time too. That type of thing happened more than once and began to occur regularly.

As I continued therapy, I was startled when I put the pieces together and understood that I was the cause of my marriage ending. The extra weight I had been carrying was a barrier to keep me safe, and I had believed I was unworthy of love.

Chapter Five

IMPACT

MY PAST COMES BACK TO HAUNT ME

One day, while sitting on that overstuffed leather couch in Penny's office for another therapy session, I began to realize that keeping myself extremely busy was my way of not having to deal with my past. Having a "suck it up, buttercup" mentality didn't help me, but rather hurt me. And although I don't recall what she asked me that day, I do remember feeling both surprise and disbelief from what unraveled in that session.

I had minimized the sexual abuse I experienced all those years ago because I had thought that, since he didn't put his penis inside me, it didn't count as sexual abuse. I had rationalized that other women who experienced rape had it way worse than I did, so I should just let it go and get over it.

"Penny, he never put his penis inside of me, so I didn't think I needed to go to therapy or deal with it," I said meekly.

She leaned forward, looked directly into my eyes, and sternly said, "Julie, he touched your body without your permission. Repeatedly. Over many years. He threatened you so you wouldn't tell anyone. That's abuse."

With my eyes open wide, I sat quietly, taking in what she said. I finally saw that my subconscious had kept me safe by minimizing my experience so I wouldn't have to deal with the fact of how gross I felt when Dan suddenly slithered his hand up my shirt and touched my bare breasts without my consent. It helped me ignore the fact that I didn't give him permission to sneakily slide his hand down my pants when we were lying on the carpeted floor in the game room in the basement at his house, or that I had to keep quiet while my brother and Dan's sister were watching the show right in front of us. It helped me block out my confusing thoughts that, even though I wasn't attracted to him like I was attracted to Tom Fletcher, maybe this was his way of showing me he liked me. Perhaps I should like him back. Perhaps I should like being touched by him, even though it made me cringe. It helped me mask the pain that it didn't seem to matter to him that I said no to him repeatedly each time I moved his hand away from my private parts.

As I continued to sit quietly, thoroughly soaking in this new awareness, I realized that minimizing, hiding, and not dealing with the sexual abuse, as if it somehow didn't matter, had negatively impacted all areas of my life. My eyes stared off, blankly out Penny's office window, and my jaw hung open as my mind slowly connected the dots. I could finally see how all the areas of my life were intertwined together.

Oh my God, I thought. *It impacted my marriage.*

And my relationships with friends.

And family.

My health.

Oh my God, even my career and money.

I silently continued connecting the dots in my mind. *Holy fucking shit. Years of stuffing my emotions and memories caused the stress and illness in my body. I did all this damage to myself by not dealing with the fucking sexual abuse!*

My shoulders slumped. I looked back at Penny with a frown on my face and tears in my eyes. She continued to hold space for me in silence, like she knew I was figuring it out.

I was reminded of a video of a colorblind father unwrapping a pair of glasses that the gleeful group highly encouraged him to put on. He put the glasses on, opened his eyes, looked around, dropped his jaw, and cried uncontrollably. The tears were joyful tears because, for the first time in his life, he could see all the glorious colors around him. He saw the skin, eye, and hair color of his beautiful daughter. He saw the bright pink peonies, green blades of grass, and billowing white clouds in the blue sky. It was as if a whole new world had come alive right before his eyes—because it just did. Everything looked so completely different, and he was in awe of the splendor.

That happened to me. Only, it didn't feel bright and colorful or exciting, and my tears weren't joyful. Rather, it felt like a kick in the gut, and my tears were of pain. Now I could see clearly how my past had impacted my whole life. I could see that I had unknowingly put up a wall of protection around my heart so no one could hurt me, but the kicker was it also blocked anyone from fully getting to know me.

More tears welled up in my eyes as the truth cleverly unfolded like the revealing of the secret to a magic trick. With these new "awareness glasses" on, I could see I was a thick, hard-covered, closed book with an invisible lock on it, and I didn't share diddly-squat with people. I was too afraid to share many of my thoughts and feelings because if I did, I might get hurt. People might judge me or tell others my secrets. I had closed my heart off and blocked people from getting in, all to protect myself. I had been afraid to be me. Without realizing it, I had been afraid to let people who care about me see the real me for all those years.

It was all starting to make more sense. Pneumonia, gluten intolerance, the tumor in my uterus, the extreme exhaustion, the struggles with extra weight—all those symptoms were evidence that the stuffed emotions stemming back to childhood traumas and sexual abuse were the cause. It was confusing, though, to connect those dots because I had to recognize the beliefs I had held to be true up until that point weren't valid. It felt kind of like the time I was first told Santa Claus wasn't real. I was shocked and couldn't believe trusted adults had tricked me into believing something that wasn't true, but at the same time I had already had a sense inside that Santa wasn't a real person. As I looked back at times I wondered if Santa was real, it all seemed to make more sense that he wasn't, and it answered all the open questions in my mind.

That's what it was like for me to understand the impact on my health from not dealing with my personal emotional baggage (aka crap). So many things I had learned from the so-called experts and had believed to be true weren't entirely accurate, like the common belief that eating healthy and exercising are *the* answers to losing weight. The truth is, they are only part of the equation in dealing with the symptoms of excess weight. If we don't deal with the actual cause— stuffed and stuck emotions from one or more upsetting life situations—then the weight will pile back on with a vengeance. I know that painfully well now from my weight loss roller-coaster ride. The other illnesses I had experienced in my body were from not effectively processing all of my emotions during or after stressful life experiences but burying them alive instead.

And I unexpectedly saw how this behavior had affected my marriage. My jaw dropped open as I suddenly I realized just how much fault I shared with my ex-husband. I looked at Penny and said, "It was my fault my marriage ended in divorce." I paused as I swallowed an air bubble filled with pride, then quietly continued. "Even though my husband cheated on me."

She looked into my eyes and nodded to affirm my understanding.

We sat in silence for a few moments as I counted back the years to realize how long we were divorced. "It's been fifteen years since we got divorced, Penny, and I am just now realizing I significantly contributed to our failed marriage." Looking down at the floor, I continued speaking in just above a whisper. "It was easier to blame him for our marriage ending because he cheated on me than it was for me to take full responsibility for my part in it."

I paused, looked up at Penny, and looked back down as I continued. "But the truth was, our marriage fell apart long before he cheated on me."

After another pause, I said, "Even though I had admitted to people I contributed to our communication deteriorating, in my mind I still blamed him." Tears dropped onto the floor.

Penny quietly held space for me as I paused again while I continued to make links back to the cause. "Frankly, our marriage was destined for divorce from the beginning, because I didn't know I needed to deal with my past and didn't have any intention of doing so. I thought it was better to leave it buried and not talk about it to anyone. Ever."

I shook my head as I processed my new reality. "It didn't feel safe for me to open up my heart to anyone fully, so I never really, truly opened up to my husband. He never even got the chance to wholly and intimately know the real me." I took in another big breath and continued. "Heck, I didn't even know the real me. It makes me so sad. I see how much I lived in fear."

There it was, plain as day. The dissolution of my marriage was my fault. My freaking fault!

On the one hand, it was a bitter pill to swallow, and I felt horrible knowing we never had a chance, no matter how hard he had tried. On the other hand, I felt the relief of revealing the truth to myself.

Penny suggested I journal about how I felt, and that I consider writing my ex-husband a letter. When she saw me cringe, she assured me I wouldn't have to give it to him. But my cringe wasn't at the thought of giving him the letter. It was the fact that I would have to admit I was wrong and apologize on paper after blaming him for all of those years.

APOLOGIES

To be brutally honest, back then I didn't have a very good opinion of men. Unless they were a family member, I believed that men only wanted one thing from me, and one thing only: *Sex.*

That was it. I couldn't see men for more than sex. I whittled my idea of relationships with men down to just that, even though I craved a much deeper connection. I had proof that helped me form that belief. Starting back in sixth grade, my boyfriend broke up with me because I wouldn't kiss him. Then Dan repeatedly and aggressively touched my private parts whenever he wanted. And between seventh and tenth grade, at least ten different guys made it known they wanted to have sex with me. Even a manager at work wanted me to come into work early in the morning before everyone else so I could have sex with him in the back room. The messages I heard from guys about how girls should behave were mixed. If we didn't do what they wanted, then we were prudes. If we did what they wanted, then we were sluts. I didn't have sex with all those guys because I didn't want to be a slut and wasn't interested in them, including the manager. But I did have sex with a few of the ones I liked because I didn't want to be a prude, and I wanted them to love me. I thought love and sex were the same thing. There was a fine line that felt confusing and shameful, especially having grown up Catholic.

Fast-forward to more proof when I was nineteen years old. Five of my guy "friends" had a contest to see who could land me first after my boyfriend and I had just broken up. I wasn't interested in any of them and turned them away repeatedly.

That's when my future husband, Dave, walked into my life. But I was so jaded that it took him three asks before I said yes to a date with him. Thankfully, he was persistent. I found there was something different about him. He treated me well, wanted to spend lots of time with me, and seemed interested in getting to know me. He wasn't just after sex. But six years after we married, despite recently having our son, we didn't spend a lot of time together. After a long day at work, making dinner, feeding our son, taking care of him, and putting him to bed, I was exhausted. Dave often came home after a busy day at work and wanted to be intimate with me. I felt depleted from giving so much to everyone else and so disconnected from him that I just couldn't. I wanted him to sit down on the couch next to me, hold my hand, and ask me about my day. He tried to connect too, but in a different way. I said no to him multiple times and thought, *He's just like the rest of them.* In hindsight, I can see how he must have felt rejected by his wife. If only I had opened up more to let him know how I was feeling and what I needed. If only I had made time for the two of us instead of giving to everyone else.

Since I didn't believe that a man could want a relationship deeper than sex, I could now also see why I had been single the majority of years since my divorce.

That evening after therapy, I figured I might as well take Penny's advice and spend a couple of hours processing this crap, since this new realization was taking on a life of its own in my head. It was as if I were at the end of my life, and my mind was going back through different memories of the life I had lived, but it was looking at them with my new awareness glasses on.

As each memory resurfaced, I was able to see it from a new standpoint. I took out my journal and wrote down all the ways the abuse had impacted my life. I drafted a letter to Dave about how the effects of this trauma affected our marriage. As I wrote, I crossed out words and sentences and rewrote the letter multiple times before I felt satisfied that I had clearly articulated myself. With each new draft, I took a little more responsibility for my part in our failed marriage. With each rewrite, I felt more in alignment with my truth and more relief inside my body. I could even breathe deeper down into my belly.

I didn't plan on giving the final version of the letter to him, but something inside me was urging me to speak to him. I remembered when Bobby told me she felt compelled to talk to her uncle, who had sexually abused her. She said it was a feeling inside her that she couldn't explain or help others understand. I understood that feeling now. I wanted to apologize to Dave. I sensed that it was essential to have that conversation together, in person.

The best way I can describe that sense is by comparing it to a craving. Have you ever craved pizza or ice cream so much that you went out of your way to drive to the store or restaurant to get it, even though it was late and you were in your comfy clothes? And you realized what you were doing was kind of crazy, but you couldn't seem to stop yourself even though you weren't necessarily hungry and you knew you might regret it later? It's kind of like that. But the intensity of the urge to talk to Dave was a gentler, calmer, persistent sense compared to a screaming ice cream craving that demanded I eat some right now so I could find temporary relief from the emotion I was avoiding. Instead, that urge to apologize to Dave quietly and patiently took up residence in my mind, waiting for an opportune time to present itself so I could find permanent relief from feeling the emotions I had been avoiding. What a dichotomy.

It turned out I wouldn't have to wait long to have that conversation. Just three days later, I was feeling happy and content after visiting with my ninety-two-year-old Grandma Bonnie. My radio was blasting to cover up my out-of-tune singing on my drive back to the Twin Cities from nearby Rochester, Minnesota, where Grandma Bonnie lived. I would be driving by the semitruck garage (aka "the shop"), where

Dave rented space to park and do maintenance and repairs on his semitrucks. My son, Craig, who was now sixteen years old, was with his dad; I knew he was planning to be at the shop to work on his pickup truck sometime that weekend. I called Craig to let him know I would be passing by the shop, and he invited me to stop in to see him. I thought he was alone. When I walked into the shop, Dave rolled out on a flat scooter board from underneath his semitruck and said, "Hello, Julie."

I was surprised. *Oh no,* I thought. *I'm not ready to see Dave today. Do I say something now?*

I looked around the shop. No one else was there. Here it was, the perfect moment. I had to say something.

How do I do this? I asked myself. *Speak from your heart, Julie. You can do this.*

In a split second, my mind flipped back to the moment I shared my story onstage. I reminded myself of the freedom and connection I felt afterward.

With a little crack and fumble in my voice, I asked, "Dave, did Craig mention I am in therapy for sexual abuse from my past?"

"Yeah, he mentioned something about it," he confirmed quietly. "I remember you shared with me about the abuse one time when we were first dating, and you never brought it up again."

I nodded. "I didn't realize how much the sexual abuse neg- atively impacted me until after working with my therapist on the abuse memories that were popping into my mind. That is when I realized I was never able to fully open up to you, Dave, and realized my fault in our divorce. I am so sorry."

We stared at each other in silence. It was a surreal moment,

standing in a dirty shop next to a semitruck with tears streaming down my face, in conversation with my ex-husband about
something so personal that had happened so many years
before. Time stood still in that uncomfortable and awkward
moment. But at the same time, it was a heartfelt and appro-
priately huggable and healing moment. He looked down to
see a big grease spot covering most of the front of his white
T-shirt, and silently we agreed not to hug.

I must have had those awareness glasses on again because,
at that moment, I seriously felt my heart expand for Dave in
a new way that I hadn't ever felt with anyone. Somehow I instantly knew, saw, and felt that Dave had tried so hard to love
me as long as he could despite my history, baggage, and im-
perfections, but I didn't wholly allow his love in. I felt sadness
for him because he was kept at arm's length by his wife. Me.

My apology wasn't an attempt to get back together, nor
was it sexual in any way. It was about opening up my heart
and apologizing to him for my part in our marriage ending. It
was about both of us releasing the past, letting go, and accepting what was and what is. As our conversation continued,
we both agreed that we still didn't belong together, and life
had turned out as it was supposed to.

As I drove home, I felt the remaining sorrow release as the
tears dripped off my face, soaked into my teal cotton capris,
and transformed into feelings of joy and freedom. The truth
was out, I could see clearly, and I felt the relief of it all inside
my body.

The very next afternoon, I reported back to Penny that I
had apologized to my ex-husband in person and shared how
good I felt afterward. I think she was surprised that I had taken
action so quickly after we had talked about it the Thursday

before because she had that wow-stunned look on her face, but her smile indicated she was also very proud of me.

I was proud of myself too. I knew that working through all this and letting go of my baggage would help me be open-hearted in my future relationships with significant others.

Chapter Six

THE MIND-
BODY CONNECTION

DR. ANGIE

While I was trying to go to therapy as much as possible before my therapist moved away, I was still going to my chiropractor twice a week. But it wasn't until the week after my last day of therapy that I discovered just how these two very different methods of healing overlapped.

The Monday morning following my last day of therapy, while getting ready to head back to work full-time, I was bending forward to put on my pants when my lower back went out. The intense pain took my breath away. I was in a bent-over position, with my pants halfway up, and I couldn't move. I was stuck and wasn't sure what to do because any slight movement caused intense pain to shoot through my body.

Oh, this is just fucking great, I thought. *My first day back to work full-time, and my back goes out. What should I do? Should I call in? Yeah, right. What the hell would I say? I can't get my pants up, so I can't come in? I can't call in sick. It's my first day back full-time. This should make for a fun day. Thank God I have a chiropractor appointment over lunch hour. And thank God this happened after I showered and styled my hair. How the hell am I going to get dressed now?*

I gradually lowered my body onto the carpeted floor in

my bedroom. While taking in the deepest breath that I could muster, I guided my body to lie down and relax into the floor.

Okay, you can do this, I thought. *Take a deep breath in. Let go. Relax right into the floor, just like you learned in that yoga class. C'mon, body. You can do this.*

After a few minutes, my body loosened up enough that I could ever so slowly move into an upright position without wanting to scream from the pain. But when I looked in the mirror, I saw my body was noticeably leaning off to the left side. I tried to straighten it out, but I stopped after wincing in pain.

After managing to get my clothes all the way on, I navigated my way down each step and into the garage. I drove to work, and when it was time to get out of the car, my body felt even stiffer than it had at home just forty-five minutes earlier. Every little movement caused a lightning bolt of pain to shoot up my spine. I paused to think about which part of my body I should move first to feel the least amount of pain. I slowly rotated toward the open car door, put my feet on the ground one at a time, and stood up at a snail's pace. It wasn't an easy task. When I stood in an upright position, I felt absolutely ridiculous knowing I had to walk into the office because I thought I looked like one of those short, hunched-over monkeys from *The Wizard of Oz.*

I wanted to cry from the intensity of the pain and the fact that I had to deal with this, and I knew I couldn't possibly wait until lunch hour to get adjusted. I needed help and relief ASAP. After changing my appointment, I canceled all my evening plans for the week, because I knew this wasn't a quick fix and that I needed to support my body's healing process, just as Penny had taught me.

Thank goodness I had been getting chiropractic adjustments from Dr. Angie for the previous seven months, and
she knew how my body responded to being adjusted. I had
initially started going to Dr. Angie in January that year after
my nutrition coach referred me for the third time. I finally
listened. I had been struggling with my weight, digestion, and
breathing; and I didn't seem to be making a lot of headway
improving those issues despite significantly changing my food
and supplement intake. The symptoms had gotten worse as
I'd made changes to my diet. My stomach had become even
more bloated, and I would rush to the bathroom more frequently. Plus, my tongue would get tingly, and my lips would
go numb when I ate certain fruits and vegetables like avoca-
dos and tomatoes. My body had become increasingly sensi-
tive, my food frustration had intensified, and I was struggling
with what step to take next. I preferred to help my body heal
through more natural solutions, knowing our bodies are built
to heal themselves. I had previously had good experiences
with chiropractors, so I thought it was a good next step.

I didn't know this in advance of working with Dr. Angie,
but her chiropractor training allowed for support with deeper
and longer-term emotional stressors like sexual abuse. She
is a neurological chiropractor. The majority of chiropractors
learn what's called *diversified technique,* which is a structural
technique. A chiropractor who takes additional courses to
learn neurological techniques is trained to adjust the areas
that have the most influence on the nervous system. Instead
of adjusting bone to muscle to nerve, the neurological chiropractor adjusts from the inside out in the reverse order, from
nerves to muscle to bone. The idea is to unwind the nervous
system and then let the body do the rest.

When Dr. Angie first saw me, she looked me up and down and inquired, "Wow, Julie, what have you done?"

I laughed as I told her, "I put on my pants."

She chuckled and then asked me to lie down on the black, upholstered chiropractic table with my face in the cradle. I felt awkward and dorky and was even a little embarrassed because of all the time and effort it had taken me to bend down low enough to be able to maneuver my body onto the table. Even though I was in pain, we laughed at the situation, and then I half-jokingly whined because it hurt to laugh.

My lower back was what hurt, but she started adjustments on the occiput, which is the bone at the base of the head. Then she adjusted the sacrum, which is the triangular bone that attaches to the tailbone. She explained the occiput and the sacrum work together when we breathe, pumping the cerebral spinal fluid up the spine and back down again. When someone is going through a stressful situation and isn't processing their emotions effectively, it puts stress on the body. When the body is stressed, if the sacrum and occiput get stuck, they twist and rotate, which puts the whole body in fight-flight-freeze mode (aka the sympathetic state). I'm pretty sure I had a confused look on my face as I tried to follow along with all the technical jargon.

Dr. Angie must have realized that, because she grabbed a rubber band to show me an example to help me understand what was happening inside my body. She pulled the rubber band tight and twisted it in the center. I noticed the twist extended to the top and bottom of the rubber band, not just the center where she had twisted it. She said that I had a huge global twist throughout the entire spinal system, not just down by my sacrum. Under normal circumstances, when she adjusted the occiput and sacrum, it would untwist the body like a rubber band untwisting. That day, my body was still stuck, and it took five adjustments before my system started to loosen and unwind.

Dr. Angie had a big smile on her face because she was excited to see how my body would shift throughout the week. She often had a hard time getting patients to understand the mind-body connection because many people disassociate their physical body from their mental and emotional feelings. They don't understand that their mind and body strategically work together and that not processing their emotions effectively in daily life as well as challenging situations can result in physical body pain.

This was a topic Dr. Angie and I were both fascinated with. We had some rather dynamic conversations during my appointments, as we were intrigued about how each other's work related to this connection between emotions and bodily pain. Although I had zero desire to have in-depth knowledge about the spinal structure like she did, I did have a curiosity about how the adjustments helped my body get unstuck so it could go back to healing itself. Plus, I was quite intrigued by how the body could be adjusted in one area and feel it in a completely different area. I loved seeing how much Dr. Angie was captivated and delighted by the body. Even though she had been a chiropractor for seven years, she was still like a giddy kid in the candy store, determining which type of adjustment would work best and watching the body shift after she adjusted it. I knew I was seeing the right chiropractor at the right time!

Dr. Angie knew through our conversations that I understood that connection more and more as I was going through

EFT training, and so did she. She hadn't heard of EFT before meeting me and was eager to know more about it. Since I was in the process of getting certified and needed to complete client sessions as part of my certification, we set up a group EFT session with her and her staff. I first taught them the basics about tapping and then tapped on a specific bothersome situation with each person. At the time, Dr. Angie was thirty-eight weeks pregnant with her second child and was a bit nervous about labor contractions. As we tapped, she recalled being incredibly annoyed by the contractions with her first child and wasn't looking forward to going through that again. In the group, we tapped on that memory, accompanying emotions and sensations in her body. Fast-forward to two weeks later, after Dr. Angie's labor, and she was amazed that she had gone through every contraction without feeling annoyed at all.

The majority of people usually try to figure out an external reason for the cause of pain in their body, like I used to do. Most of their most significant stressors are not the physical stressors put on their body from movement or lifting, but rather the mental and emotional stressors we create with our thoughts alone. Reread that last sentence. It's a crucial message to take in. We create stress in our bodies with the thoughts we think and by not fully processing our emotions.

When she finished adjusting, I carefully maneuvered my way back off the table and stood up as straight as my body would allow, which was a little straighter than when I had arrived. I let out an audible sigh of relief but was a bit disappointed that I still felt severe pain, even though I knew it could be several days before my body felt total relief. I just hoped it would be sooner than later.

When I stood up out of bed on Thursday morning, I felt elated. I was only slightly leaning to the left. *Thank God! Body, you're AWESOME! I am feeling so much better.* Sitting in the car made my back feel worse like it had the other days, and I continued ice and heat with a funny duck-quacking alarm making me laugh and alerting me to rotate every twenty minutes.

My chiropractic appointment was after work that day. When Dr. Angie was moving my feet to determine where she was going to adjust, I felt other parts of my body shifting and moving even before she made an adjustment. She started adjusting my back and was extra-excited to see my body's progress on the fourth day. She could tell my body had released enough of the superficial stuff that caused the awful pain because it was allowing her to adjust a deeper layer of the nervous system.

Dr. Angie explained, "Not only were you not well neurologically in the upper digestive system, where food starts to get digested, you were also holding onto it instead of letting go and eliminating it." But the way she could tell I was working on letting go of things was that my body only needed three adjustments that day. That was a significant change, and evidence that my body was strengthening enough to heal on its own.

BLAMING THE DAMN FOOD

Ding, ding, ding. *Oh my gosh!* The bell went off in my head as another puzzle piece clicked into place. Between what I had learned in EFT classes, going through therapy, conversations with Dr. Angie, and all the mindset training from Dr. Wayne Dyer, Abraham Hicks, and Louise Hay, I got the full picture.

All these years, my body has been working so hard to keep me safe, and my digestive system shut off because my body was in fight-flight-freeze mode, I thought. *No wonder I had so many upset stomachs and had to rush to the bathroom so much. My body was highly stressed—every day. And it couldn't process food too. All because I shut down and didn't deal with my emotions and thoughts from the sexual abuse stuff. My stomach got worse and worse over the years, especially during the time I was struggling financially. I blamed food for my sick feeling and upset stomach. Holy shit!*

Most recently, I had pinned it on gluten and dairy for causing my upset tummy issues. Blaming something outside me only made it worse. I created beliefs that it was their fault, and my subconscious latched onto these beliefs and made them real.

Especially over the past few years, food had been so frustrating to me. First of all, I didn't like to cook or bake anymore. But I obviously needed food to stay alive, so I needed to cook. I felt so limited in what I could eat because I thought gluten and dairy didn't agree with my tummy. They are ingredients in many of the foods I often ate, so I felt deprived that I couldn't eat those foods. Most of the time, I didn't know what to eat anymore. There were hundreds of books by authors touting their answers for the right way to eat. But each one's approach was the opposite of the others' methods, so I didn't know which one was right. I was angry I had to switch my diet and check all the damn ingredients before eating anything—meanwhile other people could eat whatever the hell they wanted without getting sick or gaining weight. And restaurants . . . don't get me started. I dreaded them, even though at that point I wanted someone else to cook for me so I wouldn't have to hassle with it. They had hardly anything on the menu that I could eat. Nothing was labeled gluten- or dairy-free back then, and it seemed like a big ordeal if I asked about options. Arrrrrgh. It was so frustrating!

I took the time to grasp how I was training my mind to get sick if I ate gluten and dairy so I could stop doing that and change my thinking to something more powerful. The truth for me was, I didn't have a physical intolerance to gluten and dairy. Instead, my intolerance to them was caused by emotional associations with those foods and the beliefs I created around them.

My digestive system wasn't working correctly in the first place because of being in fight-flight-freeze mode for so long. But then I made it worse with my negative thoughts and emotions about food, specifically dairy and gluten. Inadvertently, I had trained my stomach to get upset more often. When I ate food, no matter what it was, I was putting anger and frustration into my body. And afterward, I had to rush to the bathroom as my body relieved itself of the angry and frustrating food I had just consumed and couldn't digest, but I blamed it on dairy and gluten. The more frequently I got sick, the more upset I got about food, and the more I blamed what I ate.

Here's what happened: I created a belief that gluten and dairy made me sick by repeatedly saying out loud to others with great emotion that I couldn't eat them and emphasizing how sick I got afterward if I did eat them. I was quite adamant about it. My body did exactly as I had instructed. It got sick whenever I ate gluten or dairy, whether I was aware that the food contained them or not. That's how the subconscious mind works. It takes on messages from ourselves and others as truth and behaves accordingly; and when intense emotions couple with thoughts, the subconscious acts even quicker. The subconscious runs the show, and we can't change it until we become aware of our beliefs. Thankfully, I understood what I had unknowingly created and was ready to start making changes to help my body heal.

On Friday morning, I woke up feeling so much better, and I didn't look like an Oz monkey anymore. *Hallelujah!* I only had a little bit of pain in my lower back and could stand up much straighter. I felt relief and was in awe of how quickly my body was healing. When I arrived at Dr. Angie's office, I was able to get out of my car faster than a snail without feeling much pain.

Dr. Angie adjusted two places in my lower back and then apologized before she told me where she had to adjust next. She prefaced it by saying it would be a little uncomfortable because she needed to adjust my pubic bone. I laughed and said, "Of course you do. I was doing therapy for childhood sexual abuse. That totally makes sense."

In therapy, I had finally opened up about some of the most traumatic and vulnerable experiences in my life after keeping them to myself for over thirty years. Adjusting my pubic bone felt like an appropriate and funny last adjustment to help heal that part of my past. And I felt relief in that entire area of my body afterward.

She nodded and told me that the pubic bone often ties emotionally to events like sexual abuse, having a baby, or moments of extreme vulnerability. She freqently adjusted post-partum moms there because they had just gone through one of the most vulnerable moments of their life when a baby came through their pelvis. She pointed out that it doesn't have to be traumatic in a negative way, but it's often vulnerability on the mental and emotional side of things that still has to be worked through to heal fully.

I knew from EFT certification that emotions are trapped in the body, because I'd felt relief from pain in my body after tapping. But it wasn't until that week, between the extreme pain and the conversations with Dr. Angie, that I fully grasped how any physical symptoms we experience in our bodies are a result of emotions trapped in them. It was like the splinter Penny had talked about. When we don't process all the emotions, they fester and cause pain in our bodies.

Feeling the physical pain, discerning where the associated emotions stem from, and understanding how the body functions helped me comprehend and appreciate the mind-body connection. No longer was the "mind-body connection" a superficial spiritual phrase to me. It was now a deep knowing.

PART TWO

finding
my voice

Chapter Seven

WORTHY

FEELING UNWORTHY

I had worked with Integrative Life Coach and Hay House author Nancy Levin the previous year in her first Jump Coaching Group. Doing the work in her program helped me make some significant shifts in my life. So when she emailed me as one of her handpicked VIP clients, inviting me to participate in a special group coaching program while she was writing her next book on worthiness, it was an easy decision. Her book would help readers with their self-worth, which would help increase their net worth, which was a topic of interest and area I wanted to change in my life. I didn't need to close my eyes or check in any further with my intuition, because I already knew it was a loud and clear "YES!" I jumped at the chance to work with Nancy in a group again and signed up within a few hours of receiving the email invitation. It felt like a godsend to me.

The course arrived at the perfect time, because I was in the middle of some more major life changes and was wobbling inside about my abilities. I had decided to get certified as a financial coach with financial guru Dave Ramsey and get certified as an EFT practitioner through EFT Universe after closing my jewelry business. I knew I needed to do some personal work on my crappy beliefs around worthiness and my ability to help others in this new coaching career.

Both Patti, who I met in the EFT certification class, and I were committed to tapping together to meet the required personal tapping hours for the EFT certification and continuing to do our personal work. For one of our sessions, we met at a popular local coffee shop at a location that had a meeting room where we could tap together behind a closed door. The meeting room had a rectangular, dark brown, wooden table with deep grooves in it that made it look slatted. Six dark, earthy green wooden chairs surrounded the table. Patti's back faced the dry-erase board, and she was tucked out of sight from others in the coffee shop. I was facing the dry-erase board and positioned where people could potentially see me if they looked in the room's window or door. I felt a little self-conscious about people looking in at me, especially when I was tapping on the top of my head, but not self-conscious enough to stop tapping.

Initially, I shared with Patti that I wanted to tap on money-related stuff in preparation for the money workshop I would be leading in a couple of months. I used the word "worthy" a few times as I talked, mostly because the name of the group I was taking part in with Nancy Levin was the Worthy Coaching Group. I was surprised when Patti said she could hear something in my voice when I said the word. I was positive that I was stepping into my worthiness and that there wasn't an issue with it. But Patti's eyebrows were raised, and her head tilted to the left. She didn't have to say another word; I knew what she was saying to me by her look alone.

"Okay," I said. "I will trust you. You're the EFT practitioner. I will tap on 'worthy.'"

We started off measuring how true the statement "I am worthy" was for me on a scale of zero to ten. The number six popped into my mind. I also measured the contradictory statement "I am not worthy," and it came up as a four on a zero-to-ten scale.

We tapped argument-style, where we voiced both sides of the issue, often in a humorous way. While alternating the phrases "I am worthy" and "I am not worthy" with sarcasm in my voice, memories popped into my mind. I let them flutter on through, and it felt like they were moving out of my head as I let them go. I yawned some of the longest and widest jaw-opening yawns I've ever yawned in my life. I knew that was a sign I was clearing something profound, because when I previously yawned deep while tapping, a big realization came to me moments after.

The first time we stopped to remeasure my truth of the "I am worthy" affirmation, the number increased one point to a seven, which seemed minimal compared to how I felt inside. It felt like I was standing in a beautiful field of flowers, and a beam of sunlight was radiating on me. Something was profoundly shifting.

"Can we keep tapping on this, Patti?" I asked excitedly. "This feels sooooo good. I want to get to 'I am worthy' at a level ten. Let's keep going! Let's keep going!"

I wanted to feel what a ten felt like, because as my number increased just a bit, I felt substantially better. I noticed I no longer gave a hoot if people saw me through the glass door, tapping. The new thoughts and sensations I was feeling in my body felt so good; it just didn't matter to me what others thought if they saw me tapping on my head and face. I knew what I was doing was working.

We kept tapping and remeasured how true the affirmation was for me a couple more times. Each time I remeasured, I felt so different, but the word "better" isn't a strong enough word to even begin to describe how I felt. Patti said my shoulders and face looked lighter and freer each time my belief number increased. We tapped until I reached a ten and truly believed I was worthy. I continued to be amazed at how tapping on specific points on the body while speaking words out loud helped me feel so much better. It even opened my mind to new and uplifting thoughts. I didn't realize I needed to tap on "I am worthy," but Patti heard extra emphasis in my voice when I said the word "worthy." I could have easily glossed over it, and I even tried to! But her look told me to stick with it, and I'm glad I did. *This tapping thing is so cool,* I thought.

This time, I could feel my face light up as I said, "I am worthy." I could even hear the truth of that statement with strength and confidence in my voice. My hands gestured up in the air over my head, emphasizing the statement, "I am worthy—I am so fucking worthy!" My body aligned with it, and it felt so incredibly true. I don't know how to put into words the profound feeling I felt inside that day, but it was a whole new level of worthiness.

After tapping, it felt like I was now running, not just standing, through that beautiful field of flowers with my arms spread wide open, and a beam of sunlight was radiating on me while shouting to the world, "I am worthy." I absolutely knew, without a doubt, that I was worthy just because I was me. I danced my way out of the coffee shop and joyfully floated to my car. I knew I looked a little goofy, but I didn't care—in fact, I laughed at myself. Patti laughed with me (or maybe at me).

I was so flipping excited about how amazingly worthy I felt that I wanted everyone to feel that way and experience the fantastic shift and change that I experienced. I asked Nancy Levin if I could offer to tap with the Worthy Coaching Group. We set up a group session to tap on "I am worthy" together over the phone, and it impacted others profoundly too.

CALM, CONFIDENT, AND GRATEFUL

Four months later, I had a chance to apply my new level of worthiness to my income. I was in a quandary about my salary from my job. Although I was grateful to be earning more money than I ever had before, I felt like my responsibilities and skills continued to increase exponentially. Still, the compensation didn't increase proportionately with the role expansion.

When I was organizing documents on the confidential drive at work, I came across salary information for the person that was in the role before me. Their salary was over $140,000 more per year than what I was making. Although my skill set was different and some of the responsibilities were different than those of the previous person in that role, it led me to do further research for comparable positions outside the company, including salaries and skill sets. I concluded that I wanted to ask for a raise, but I just wasn't sure how to clearly articulate what I wanted and knew I needed to take time to get clear before I could request such a raise.

During my next one-on-one coaching session with Nancy Levin, we talked about the raise I wanted to ask for. She asked me why I was giving a range of $20,000 to $30,000 and said I needed to get clear on what I wanted and ask for a specific dollar amount instead of a range.

After we got off the phone, I took time to get clear for

myself. I needed first to be able to articulate to myself exactly what I was asking for and why I was asking for it so I could gain confidence. I sat down with a pen and paper and focused on identifying reasons why I had already earned the raise without fixating on the fact that I was making less than other comparable positions. I wrote down my logical reasons for requesting an increase. My list included work efficiencies, significantly reducing business expenses, a high level of service, continuous improvement in communications and teamwork, and a willingness and ability to learn whatever my boss needed me to so I could serve him better.

Once I figured out why I wanted a raise and the value I offered to my boss, it was time for me to figure out what to say.

I stopped to think about how I wanted to FEEL during my conversation. I pulled out my journal to first write out how I didn't want to feel inside. I listed fears I had about asking for the raise. It sounds funny that I listed out what I don't want, but the thoughts and concerns were in my head. I needed to get them out. Plus, I've found that I get a lot of clarity when I list out what I don't want, then I flip the question to ask myself, "What *do* I want?" I listed out several options like *happy, calm, joyful, peaceful, excited, amazed, proud,* confident, grateful, and *cheerful.*

Just like trying on clothes for their fit and feel, I tried on the different emotions. Then I asked myself, *Does it fit? Does it feel good? Is that how I want to feel in this meeting? Is it appropriate?*

I didn't want to feel anxious, have sweaty palms, or stumble over my words. I wanted my body to feel peace and calm so I could speak easily. I paused to feel calmness inside my body. My tummy felt at ease, and my mental chatter stopped.

This feels good, I thought. *I choose "calm" for my first word. Hmmm, how else do I want to feel?*

I tried on *excited* to feel how that felt in the meeting. I closed my eyes, imagining where I sat, started a conversation, and felt excited. I realized it felt similar to anxious, and it didn't pair well with calmness. I crossed off *excited* and asked myself, *What do I want to feel with "calm"?* The word confi-dent popped up in my mind. *Yes! Confident.*

I wanted to be that confident leader I was while asking for the raise. And it does take confidence to be able to ask for a raise, no matter how much. Sitting up in my chair with my shoulders back and a calm feeling in my tummy, I took a deep breath in; and as I exhaled, I felt good about my feeling choices of calmness and confidence. *Anything else, Julie? Anything else you want to feel in that meeting?* Immediately the word *gratitude* popped into my mind. *Ahhhh, yes.* I smiled. *Gratitude. That's it!* I exclaimed in my head.

I wanted to feel gratitude going into that meeting. I knew going into my annual review discussion that I would likely receive another $5,000 raise, as I had the past couple of years. Each time I received that $5,000 raise, I felt gratitude. It was very generous. I closed my eyes as my mind continued on a rant of appreciation about other things I was grateful for. *I am grateful to be employed. Grateful to have this opportunity. Grateful for all the experiences I get because I work with Doug. I have met so many people and had conversations I would have never been a part of if I weren't working for him.* I felt tears forming behind my eyelids and continued the rant in my head. *I am grateful for the learning and growth opportunities I get in addition to classes and workshops.* My smile expanded across my face. *I get to be a part of strategic investment and tax planning conversations. I get to see how he makes deci-sions. I am grateful for the opportunity to continue working with him for years to come. And I am very grateful to receive any amount for a raise.*

I soaked in the feeling of gratitude with deep breaths and felt my heart expand open. *Yes, grateful is how I want to feel. I am ready. Calm, confident, and grateful are the emotions I will feel during the meeting.*

The next step was to set the exact dollar amount I wanted to request and then remove any attachments to achieving that exact outcome. To receive a higher raise, I first had to open myself to the possibility of receiving more. I started tap-ping on the top of my head while asking myself a lot of ques-tions to get clarity.

Would I be happy if I gave a range of twenty to thirty thou-sand dollars and received twenty? Would I be okay receiving a $20,000 raise? Do I want a $30,000 raise? Is this more in alignment with me? That last question really meant, "Am I worthy of this raise?"

While I tapped through the points and noticed how I felt inside, I talked through a couple of scenarios out loud. "If I ask for a thirty-thousand-dollar raise and my boss says no to thirty thousand dollars but yes to twenty thousand dollars, would I be okay?" After several minutes of tapping and talking, it became clear to me that I was worthy, and I was "comfort-able" with the uncomfortableness of asking for a $30,000 raise, even with all possible outcomes of that request.

After determining all that, I then practiced out loud my conversation with him. At first, it was hard and uncomfort-able, and my voice sounded mousy. Still, I practiced again and again until I felt not only comfortable on the inside but also confident with delivering the conversation out loud.

The review day arrived, and before the meeting I sat down in one of the brown padded lounge chairs in the back corner of my office, where no one could see me if they walked by. I closed my eyes, took a couple of deep breaths, and focused my intention on feeling calm, confident, and grateful in my body. I visualized the conversation with Doug. I stood up and, for a couple of minutes, held my arms up in the air in a Y-shape, which raised the energy and supported my confident feeling. By the time the meeting arrived, I was ready. I went into the conference room and sat down in the chair at the side of the conference table to the left of Doug's usual seat. Doug then joined me. We briefly discussed my work performance throughout the year. He was pleased and offered me a $5,000 raise. I took a deep breath in and quietly encouraged myself, *Okay, Julie. Just like you practiced. You got this.* I turned my head to the right to look him in the eyes, thanked him for the raise, paused, and then asked him to consider providing me with a $30,000 increase. I articulated my reasons and let him know I wasn't expecting an answer on the spot. He could take time to think about it. I then shut up.

I learned a while back but was reminded earlier that year at the Personal Story Power workshop that silence in conversations is critical. It allows the other person quiet space to think and process what they just heard. I could see Doug's eyes move up, which is something people tend to do when they are thinking and processing information. I comfortably sat in silence, feeling grateful for this moment and proud of myself for having the courage to ask for what I wanted. When Doug spoke next, he said to me, "Yes, I can do that." I did a happy dance in my mind, and my smile expanded wide across my face. Still confident, I looked him straight in the eyes again and said, "Thank you." He told me I was welcome, and I was worth it.

It was empowering to tap on worthiness as well as prepare to ask for what I believed I was worthy of receiving. But it also made me realize I had more work to do because I still had fears of speaking my truth with other people in my life. I also struggled to say no when I didn't want to do something that someone else wanted me to do.

Chapter Eight

LINE IN THE SAND

LATE NIGHT CALLS

My mom and dad wanted a little girl and completed the paperwork through the Catholic Charities adoption agency to get on the waitlist. I was adopted when I was twenty-three days old. When I was four or five years old, my parents took me to lunch to tell me how special I was and that they had adopted me. Somehow I already knew that, but I was happy to be at lunch with just the two of them. My parents ended up getting divorced when I was six or seven years old. I lived with my mom and two brothers, and I saw my dad on the weekends and at my track meets and band concerts. My mom and I had a rocky relationship, starting when I was a bratty teen. I moved to my dad's a month after I turned eighteen. It was in my early twenties when Mom and I started improving our relationship. We shifted to more of a friendship instead of a parent-child relationship.

When I was in college, and shortly after I got married, my mom occasionally called me late in the evening when I was in bed, either winding down to sleep or already sleeping. *Oh no, something must be wrong. She must really need me if she's calling this late*, I'd think. So I would answer the phone. *I'm here for my mom. That's what a good friend-daughter does.*

After a few of these calls, I realized I felt emotionally

depleted each time I got off the phone. I would quietly listen to her vent nonstop about something she was struggling with in her life. But when she'd pause to take a breath and I'd hope to change the subject, she'd tell me instead that she was tired and had to hang up. Although I was exhausted, I wouldn't sleep because I was angry and resentful that she never even asked about me.

This didn't just happen with my mom. I noticed I seemed to get angry with people I didn't necessarily want to help but helped anyway. Worse, I felt guilty for not wanting to help some people, so I said yes anyway. But after assisting them, I often felt like I had been taken advantage of. It confused me. I thought I was supposed to be helpful and kind to everyone so we'd all get along together. Isn't helping others and compromising even when I don't want to do those things part of being the bigger person? But for some reason, I didn't feel good inside when helping others in this way. I thought if I were a good wife, a good daughter, a good friend, a good sister, a good mom, and a good employee, then everything would go well, and I wouldn't let anyone down.

But there was a problem with that. It rarely felt right for me, and I often felt let down. I was so busy trying to do what made everyone else happy that I failed to realize I wasn't happy. I just wanted to get along with everyone and please them. The more I behaved in specific ways to please them because I thought I was supposed to, the more I lost myself and the worse I felt.

What I learned over time when I started healing from childhood sexual abuse is it's a common effect not to understand boundaries or be able to say no. The abuse process impacts and interrupts normal brain growth and development, including self-esteem. It's also common to not recognize one's interests. When I understood that, it made me feel like I wasn't so alone or broken. I set out to learn about boundaries through reading books and participating in group coaching. But the most interesting way I got to learn about boundaries was through horse coaching.

HORSE COACHING

I first met Ann Romberg, who calls herself the Carrot Coach, at a workshop and heard her describe her work as a horse coach. She said the horse is the coach to her clients, and she's a partner with the horse. Her role is as an observer of the horse's behavior in response to the client. She observes their interactions and points out what the horse is doing to help the client interpret it as it applies to their life. For example, if I were in conflict with someone at work or in my personal life and needed to have a conversation with them to work through it, then I could first have a conversation with a horse to see what I needed to change based on their reaction to me.

Ann explained how the horses help coach clients in a combination of ways through their naturally intuitive behavior. They watch and sense the client's energy through their eyes, ears, nose, feet, skin, and tongue. The client may have a thought in their head that is very different from what is in their heart. The horses physically mirror back to the client what the client is doing and show them their incongruences. If what I spoke out loud didn't match what was in my heart, then the horse would mirror the disconnection to me through its behavior. It would kick its hoof in the dirt, kick its back legs up, or even back away from me. I would have to try it over again until the horse stood still or gave me a nod as if he approved of my thoughts. Working with horses provides an opportunity to practice aligning our minds and hearts in a nonjudgmental and safe way.

I was intrigued by the giant yet gentle, soulful animals. I had always loved horses, even though I didn't have much experience handling or riding them other than on a trail ride with my fifth-grade Girl Scouts troop or in Wyoming while at a family reunion on a dude ranch with real cowboys. Even though my Grandpa W. had a big barn with horses at his home in the country, I only occasionally got the chance to interact with them. When I did get the rare opportunity to feed the horses with my grandpa, I was intimidated by the horses' size and was afraid I would stand in the wrong place and get kicked.

Despite my fear and lack of horse experience, I felt an intense yearning to work with them. I wanted to work with Ann one-on-one because my leadership role at work was changing with increased responsibilities, and I needed to learn new ways to be a more effective leader. Ann created a contract, and we started working together. During my first monthly one-on-one session with the horses, I got to practice having a difficult conversation from my heart that I needed to have with an employee. It was such a cool experience for me to see how the horses interacted with me and mirrored the crap going on in my head. I got to practice speaking more authentically and knew I was on the right track with the horse's positive response, standing still and looking me in the eyes.

We first had a coaching session on the phone, where I shared a work situation with Ann. She pointed out to me that

I had a boundary issue going on at work. It was triangulation, where people were talking behind each other's backs instead of going directly to the person they needed to work the issue out with; and I felt like I was one of the targets being attacked by them. As the leader, it was my job to set appropriate boundaries with employees and provide resources to help everyone interact and work better together. Ann and I agreed to focus on understanding and setting energetic boundaries at the next in-person session with the horses.

After our call, I was feeling a little nervous and even stupid— here I was, a forty-something-year-old woman, and I didn't fully understand boundaries. I knew something was wrong because the situation felt off, and I was so uncomfortable. But I needed to understand boundaries better so I could deal with the situation more effectively to help not only myself but my employees as well. I googled boundaries and read a definition: "a line that marks the limits of an area; a dividing line."

I got it. It reminded me of the proverbial phrase "draw a line in the sand." I had done that before, so I knew I was capable of it. But I noticed I usually drew a line in the sand after feeling frustration or anger and was at the end of my rope with the situation. *How could I know to set the boundary before getting angry and reacting poorly?*

Previously when I had set boundaries, it was often met with disbelief, anger, or frustration from others. If I wasn't shown those directly to my face, then it was talked about behind my back. In some cases, both happened.

At work, because it was a family office with only a handful of employees, people could get a little too lax with their behaviors. For example, if I was working on a confidential project or making a phone call, people would sometimes walk into my office before they let me know they were there. So after a couple of employees pointed out this was also happening to them, we reviewed office etiquette in a monthly staff training together. I requested employees to pause at the door of the cube or office before entering and knock to notify their coworkers they were there. From one particular employee, that behavioral expectation was met with an eye roll and a sarcastic response of, "Isn't that a little much?" Then I wondered if I were being a bitch; I questioned my previously thought-out request and even initially felt uncomfortable enforcing it because I didn't want to upset anyone. Ultimately, everyone followed the request because I role-modeled it and others were doing it.

On my way to the horse coaching session, I drove through the country roads, turned up the gravel driveway, and parked in the grass to the left of the brick-red horse barn. I changed out of my open-toed sandals into tennis shoes so my feet wouldn't get dusty from the pasture and so I could avoid a surprising, gross squish on my bare feet if I accidentally stepped in a big clump of horse poop. I walked over to "the little house" that was built specifically for group gatherings and one-on-one sessions with horse coaches. It was a cute, cabin-like, large, open room with a small kitchen area, and off to the side were a small wooden table and four wooden chairs. It also had a living area with a couple of western-style comfy couches and padded chairs. It was a great place to congregate and talk.

Ann was already inside, waiting for me, and I could see the excitement in her twinkling eyes as she greeted me with a warm hug. She let me know how this session would work, reminding me, "The horses want to know where your energy is, meaning they want to know where your boundary begins. They will come toward you, touch you, and even gently push you until they can feel your boundary." I equated that to the personal space we experience with other humans. We have an invisible bubble around us. When someone—whether a stranger, acquaintance, or friend—gets too close to us, we feel uncomfortable and may even back away from them. We may say things like, "They are too close for comfort," or "They invaded my personal space." The horses would feel for my invisible line so they would know where my space was and when to stop.

We walked outside, unlocked the gate to get into the pasture, and headed over to the corner near a tall oak tree where all four horses were grazing. They were taking advantage of the shade the branches and leaves provided to get some relief from the hot July sun beaming down.

To start, Ann encouraged me to put an energetic boundary up around my body and approach the first horse to see what would happen. The goal was for my energetic wall to stop the horse from coming into my personal space without my permission. She again reminded me the horses were feeling for where my boundaries are, and if I didn't have them set, they would nudge me or let me know in some way.

I paused, closed my eyes, and imagined an energetic field in front of my body, extending from my neck down to my pelvis. I sighed and stepped forward to work with Victor, a beautiful, dark reddish-brown Arabian horse, Grandpa W.'s favorite kind. I could see my grandpa's face light up when he talked about Arabian horses. I could see why. Victor had an extra sparkle in his eyes. I felt a warmth in my heart as an image of my grandpa looking down at me with a proud smile as he watched me work with horses came to mind.

Victor tended to watch out for the other horses to keep them safe from any danger. He had a crooked white line from his forehead to the tip of his nose, matching his gentle but nervous and slightly high-strung personality. I was proud of the energetic field I'd set up, and confident that Victor would stay out of my personal space.

I was wrong.

Victor and I made eye contact; then he stretched out his neck, reached around my side, and gently nudged my back with his nose. I looked at Ann and started laughing. "Oh, I have to protect my backside too, huh? I just put the field up in front of me."

When we finished chuckling, she encouraged me to try again, this time putting the energetic boundary all around me, including my backside.

I closed my eyes and got re-centered, took a deep breath in, focused my attention, and imagined putting an energetic field up in front of my body and also around my backside. When I was ready, I opened my eyes, sighed, and stepped forward to work with the next horse, Cosmo. She was a saddlebred horse, usually gentle in temperament but reactive to her environment. Ann warned me she could be intrusive on boundaries. Her coat was a lighter reddish-brown compared to Victor's and had a short, white paint stripe down the center of her nose. She was one of those pissy horses that you had to watch out for so you wouldn't get kicked, but she also had a sweet side to her. I was confident I had protected myself this time, but I was wrong again.

Cosmo craned her neck to nudge my side. A little embarrassed, I laughed and looked at Ann. "Oh . . . I need to protect my sides too, not just the front and back of me."

Ann reminded me to put up an energy field all around myself, and when I was ready I would try again, this time working with Dude. I let Ann know I was up for the challenge. "Third time's a charm, right?"

Dude's coat reminded me of a first winter snow that partially dusts the brown earth with fluffy white flakes. Matching the coloring of his coat, Dude's wise, old-soul personality was very grounded. As a teacher, he teased and pushed in a not-so-subtle manner to help students understand and get the lesson. That day, his exceptional teaching skills proved consistent.

I took a deep breath in as far down in my belly as I could. When I exhaled, I closed my eyes and imagined the energy field in front of me, on my sides, and around my back. I felt confident I had it all covered this time. I took another deep breath in, let out a sigh, and stepped forward, approaching Dude. He stood still, looking at me with his wise and gentle dark brown eyes, and bowed his head down. For a brief moment, I thought I'd done it, and then he stepped forward and slightly raised his head just enough to nudge me right in the crotch gently.

Oh my God. I didn't extend the field down low enough, I thought.

And as I stood there, the memory of the guys groping me in the hallway flashed through my mind, the same one that had popped up at an inopportune time at work. I came out of my memory and back to the horse ranch to notice Dude standing with me as I let that memory go and realized why I needed to work on boundaries.

Of course I haven't had good boundaries. I barely even

understood what they were, since they had been violated and became nonexistent for me. I had a little more compassion for myself.

I looked over at Ann and shared a snippet of the memory that had flashed in my mind, feeling a little discomfort with disclosing that scene. She was kind and gentle and, in a sweet, soft voice, slowly said, "Oh Julie, I am so sorry that happened to you."

After a short, silent pause, she asked me if I was ready to try it again. I said that yes, I was; and she said that this time, I needed to put the energetic field around my whole body, not just parts of it.

"Fourth time's a charm, right?" I shook my head and groaned under my breath at my lame attempt at humor.

This time, I was even more determined to get it right. I took a deep breath in, closed my eyes, and imagined an energetic field all around me. I imagined it surrounding me from head to toe, from side to side, and from front to back. I imagined the area filled with love and light, protecting and supporting me. I opened my eyes and looked at Sis. She was the oldest horse; and despite having a lot of pain in her body, she had firm, clear boundaries. If she wanted another horse to move, they would move, and she didn't have to do much more than flick an ear to make that happen. At the same time, she was a very nurturing and grounded horse. With more certainty than the previous times, I stepped toward Sis.

She stood there. She didn't nudge my back, my crotch, my side, or anywhere else. She just stood there and nodded as if she were saying, *"You've got this."*

I proudly looked over at Ann, exclaiming, "I did it! I did it!" She cheered me on, celebrating my success. Then she asked me to reflect on what I did that time that was different compared to the other times so I would be able to repeat the process whenever I needed it.

I learned a lot about boundaries from these beautiful animals. The horses had gently nudged me where I left a hole in my energetic boundary, showing me my boundary setting has to be thorough. This also helped me understand that I need to care for my whole self, not just parts of me. I also learned it's my job to get clear with myself about the boundary I want to set, set it, and stick to it despite others trying to break it. And if initially I didn't set a clear enough boundary for myself, I could reset it.

PHONE CURFEW

After the discovery I had made during horse coaching, I asked my mom not to call me after 9:00 p.m., because I often went to bed early so I could get up at 4:00 a.m. on weekdays. She responded in frustration because she didn't like me putting parameters on when she could call me and didn't want to follow my request.

It's not that she called me every night. The late phone calls were fairly sporadic, but they negatively impacted me. I remember vividly one night when my mom called me after 11:00 p.m. When the phone rang, adrenaline rushed through my body and woke me from a sound sleep. My body shook like something was majorly wrong and went into alert mode. My mom didn't know I was sick with pneumonia, and that night I had finally been able to fall asleep. I don't remember exactly what I said when I picked up the phone, but I do know

I wasn't very kind to her. Here she was, worried about me because she hadn't heard from me, and her mom intuition was probably kicking in that I was sick. And when I picked up the phone, I yelled at her.

After that upsetting situation, I took some time to figure out a different solution, because I didn't like being woken up or how I responded. Plus, telling my mom to not call after 9:00 p.m. wasn't working, and she didn't like not being able to call when she was thinking of me. She's a night owl. I let her know she could call my cell phone at whatever time she wanted but to no longer call my home phone. I could easily put my cell phone on silent mode when I was going to bed so that the ring wouldn't bother me at times I wasn't available. That worked much better for both of us—she could call me when she was thinking about me, and I could respond when I was able.

On occasion, I broke my 9:00 p.m. rule when I answered the phone or made a call to her after 9:00 p.m. And every time afterward, I regretted it because I was often on the phone past the time I wanted to be on the phone and then got overly tired and couldn't easily fall asleep. That was my problem, not my mom's. I was the one breaking my own boundary, not her. When I realized that, I made a promise to myself that I wouldn't communicate after 9:00 p.m. even if I were wide awake. I wanted to be at my best and have the time and energy to have a positive interaction with my mom. That served both of us and was better for our relationship than if I answered with an attitude.

In reflecting on all my learnings about boundaries over the years, it was clear that frustration and anger were indicators I'd broken my boundary and needed to address it. In the past, I had thought I didn't want to be a mean bitch and set boundaries. But when I took the time to figure out what was bothering me and what I was and wasn't willing to accept from others, I found the reverse to be true. It was kind to be clear with others. I also learned I could change boundaries as needed and as I continued to grow and change.

But the biggest takeaway, and what I would call the bottom line about boundaries, is that they're about loving myself. I'm deciding what is okay and not okay for me with how others treat me and what they can expect from me when I set boundaries. The clearer I get about that for myself and others, the better I feel and the more alignment I'm in with my true, authentic self. I have learned to love boundaries.

MY HUSBAND SPOKE UP FOR ME

Back when I was married and didn't understand boundaries, I also had a hard time speaking up for myself. My former father-in-law is a very complex yet simple man. He has a creative mind that he uses in his garage workshop to create solutions to make things easier to use. He probably could make money patenting and selling some of his cool inventions. He has a big heart and often intends well, but sometimes when words come out of his mouth, they're hard to deal with and are met with awkward silence and puzzled looks.

There's also a fine line he fumbled over frequently with his cringeworthy comments to women that made me feel uncomfortable. When they were directed my way one too many times, I worked up the courage to ask my husband to talk to him. I was too scared to say something to my father-in-law myself, or even to my mother-in-law, whom I got along well with and dearly loved.

Despite my husband's conversation with his dad requesting him to cease inappropriate comments to me, my father-in-law continued. When we were alone and waiting for my husband to arrive to head to a wedding together, I was upset and shaking inside during a conversation my father-in-law initiated with me. A foot taller than me, he towered over me, but I knew I needed to speak up for myself. I put my hands up like a stop sign, backed away, and said, "No way. Don't. No. We're not talking about that."

He responded, saying he was just trying to help my sex life with my husband as if it were his business. I felt so incredibly uncomfortable with him. Although he didn't touch me, I felt my heart palpitating so fast inside, not knowing what he would do or say next. I had never felt so scared of him before.

Every time I heard a motor sound coming from the street outside, I wondered if it was my husband. Then I heard the sweet purr of his truck engine pull into the driveway. I felt relieved and safe now that he had finally arrived.

The last thing his dad said to me before my husband walked in the door was, "We can keep this secret to ourselves."

But I didn't. I privately told my husband about it after the wedding, when it was just the two of us on the ride back to his parents' house. I let him know if his dad couldn't stop himself, I would not be going to their home again, including for family holiday gatherings.

I knew that was hard on him as an only child, but I couldn't be on the receiving end of his dad's unwelcome and ungentlemanly remarks anymore. I had to draw a line in the sand to protect myself.

Dave got protectively angry for me and said he would con-front his dad in front of his mom when we got back to their house so his dad would be forced to deal with it. I could feel anxiety intensifying as it rapidly rose up inside my body from my stomach to my throat. My heart raced, and my palms were sweaty. I got scared, not because of Dave's anger but because of his parents' possible adverse reaction. I was afraid they would be upset with me, as if I had done something wrong. I felt my body fold inward and my shoulders slump forward, and I could hear my voice squeak like a child filled with fear when I told Dave I was scared. Emotions were high for all of us, ranging from embarrassment and disbelief to complete anger as we awkwardly muddled through the uncomfortable confrontation. *Oh my God! I am so scared. I just want to get the hell out of here!*

The four of us never had a quality conversation about it, but after that night the inappropriate comments stopped. I was grateful that my husband believed me and protected me. I'm sure it wasn't easy for him to have to bring that up with his parents, but through it I felt his love and support. That sit-uation helped me know I could speak up, people would hear me, and I was safe.

As I started speaking up more, I found it was easier to speak up for someone else, especially when I was angry. I didn't know I could have had some firm conversations with-out raising my voice. A few years later, after Dave and I had divorced, his parents were very involved in our son's life. Several times a year, they would take him to their cabin in the woods for the weekend. Craig loved spending time with them there, especially because he got to ride four-wheelers and snowmobiles. He loved riding anything with a motor on it. When he was two years old, I took him on his first snow-mobile ride on the unplowed street in front of our home in Stillwater, Minnesota, after a massive snowfall. He loved it and has been on a snowmobile or four-wheeler as many times as he possibly could ever since.

Craig would have rather been off riding than going to school any day. Although he liked learning subjects of interest to him and had several friends at school, he often got himself in trouble. One week had been very challenging for him, and after receiving a phone call from his second-grade teacher about his behavior, I knew I needed to find out what was going on. Following another long day at work, I picked him up at after-school care; and from the back seat of the car, in his lit-tle voice, he said he had something he wanted to tell me but couldn't. I assured him he could tell me anything at any time, just like we had talked about before. He told me he was afraid he would get in trouble if he told me. When I asked who he would get in trouble with, I was surprised he said, "Pop," his name for his grandpa on his dad's side.

After a little encouragement, Craig explained that he and Pop had been riding on a four-wheeler in the woods at the cabin when the four-wheeler tipped over onto them. I knew that Pop was very safety-conscious, especially when he was with my son, so I wasn't upset about the accident. Accidents do happen. We learn from them and do something different so we don't repeat them. But what I was angry about was that Pop had asked my son to keep that a secret from me. That was an inappropriate and heavy burden for an eight-year-old child to carry. I wasn't just angry with Pop—I was livid, and the momma bear in me was going to give him a piece of my mind.

When I confronted him, I yelled at him for telling my son to keep a secret from me because it undermined my parenting. I intentionally had specific conversations with my son so he would always know he could talk to me about anything, especially when people told him to keep a secret or not tell me something. No one had those conversations with me, and I never felt safe enough to tell anyone I experienced abuse repeatedly. Not that I thought my son would experience abuse, but I wanted him to know he was safe speaking up and I would always be there for him, no matter what.

Further, I yelled about how it had impacted Craig negatively all week at school. When a child—or an adult, for that matter—isn't equipped to handle something they're burdened with because they don't know how to deal with the emotions, it comes out sideways. For Craig, it came out in the form of getting in trouble at school.

I concluded my yelling by letting him know that if he ever did something like that again to my son, he wouldn't be taking him to the cabin again, even though my son would be upset. I wasn't threatening him. I was serious and ready to follow through for my son's sake.

I was surprised when I later found out my former father-in-law was scared of me when I yelled at him. Back then, after I heard that, I was proud that I got my message across and scared him. I used my voice and spoke up for my son. Years later, after I learned better ways to communicate, I realized I could have handled that situation a lot better without my momma-bear yelling.

Chapter Nine

SPEAKING UP

HIGH PRICE TO PAY

I can't even count how many times I've heard people say to me over the years, "You're so strong, Julie. If anyone can handle it, you can."

As a result of the challenges in my childhood, I closed off my heart and thought I had to be tough and strong to protect myself from getting hurt any further. To me, being strong meant I should handle other people's crap coming at me no matter how demanding it was. I assumed—as in, "made an *ass* out of *u* (you) and *me*"—I had to accept others' behaviors even if I was uncomfortable with it. Often I was afraid of speaking up because I didn't want to be confrontational. Nor did I want to get other people peeved at me even though I was feeling disturbed. Nine times out of ten, I didn't address my concerns with the person until after I saw them spilling over on to other people and negatively impacting them. I reasoned that if it just affected me, then I could deal with it.

After that happened a few times at work, I realized that by the time it spilled onto others, it had already gotten out of hand because I didn't take time to have a conversation to nip it in the bud when I first noticed the issue.

I had met Kit a couple of years earlier at a mutual friend's bridal shower and again at her wedding. After the wedding, we stayed connected only through Facebook. In recent months, she had made a series of poor decisions that headed her life in the way of abusing drugs and her own body after experiencing a lot of pain. She finally realized the impact of her choices and decided to make changes. I thought she was sincere, sharing that vulnerable post on Facebook and asking for employment opportunities. I needed help in my jewelry business and wanted to support her as she made changes. She worked her butt off, helping me set up displays on my table for a jewelry event; and she was appreciative of the opportunity. So I gave her more opportunities to do other work for me.

Then I asked her to work on a project at the family office for my boss, Doug. She did such a great job. I gave her more work, and Doug wanted to hire her. Even though Kit had done a great job over the last four months, initially I hesitated to hire her as an employee at the family office because I didn't fully trust her. I was a new manager at the office, and I wanted to make the right decisions. But because Doug liked her and her work, I thought maybe he had better instincts than I did. Perhaps I was being too judgmental about Kit. After all, she had proven herself, and I could mentor her. So I decided to hire her.

The first couple of months Kit was an employee, she did a great job working diligently and got a lot of work done each day. Then she had some personal issues going on in her life that she wasn't dealing with effectively. They started spilling over onto work, and she started coming in late without communicating. I talked to her about making sure she was in on time each day, mainly because I didn't want it to impact Doug, whom Kit was working on projects for. But Kit's personal drama and behaviors had already impacted me tremendously. I spent extra time and energy reaching out to her to find out if she was okay and when she'd be coming into work. Part of the point of her working there was to relieve me of stress from the heavy workload. Although she was still accomplishing tasks when she was there, her absences and lateness were becoming a big problem.

Additionally, on several days when she was at work, she spent extended periods in the bathroom. She said she was having some digestive issues, which continued for weeks. Little things kept happening that I kept talking with her about, and when she missed an important deadline, it was time to have a bigger conversation with her.

When I finally sat Kit down to formally discuss the performance issues, she confessed she had a substance abuse problem. I told her that in order to keep working at the family office, she needed to get help and show up on time for work. At first, she happily complied. But within a week or so of that conversation, Kit crossed a line that I couldn't look past. I knew if I did that, I was putting Doug—and, therefore, my job—at risk. I wasn't willing to do that.

A few days later, the human resources representative let Kit go. That set into motion a flurry of text messages and phone calls from Kit to my cell phone. In each contact, she expressed one or more emotions in an extreme manner. In different voicemails that she left just moments apart, she cried uncontrollably, laughed hysterically, and yelled loudly. She sounded crazy to me, and I didn't know what to expect next. Because of the steady stream of calls and texts with disturbing emotional responses, my body went into fight-flight-freeze mode. Each time the phone made any sound, I immediately looked over my shoulder and all around me as if she or someone else were coming to hurt me. My palms were sweaty, and I felt panicky inside and feared for my life. *This is crazy behavior. She must be doing drugs,* I thought. *I don't know what she is capable of doing. She knows where I live. She used to have a key to my home. I don't feel safe here.*

I took my son to his dad's, and when I returned home, I was greeted by a security guard that Doug had sent to pick me up. The guard drove me to downtown Minneapolis in a black sedan with tinted windows. He then checked me into a posh hotel under a different name. It felt surreal, like a scene from a movie about someone else's life.

Once settled in my room, I put my phone on silent mode and tried to calm my mind. I was utterly exhausted from all the crazy drama that had transpired over the past six hours, plus the weeks that had led up to it. I covered my eyes to sleep. That weekend, all my needs were taken care of. My only job was to relax and disconnect from the world to calm my mind and body down.

In hindsight, I saw that it was a high price to pay for not listening to my intuition and not speaking up sooner when things were starting to go wrong. It took a toll on me—physically, emotionally, and mentally. My lack of speaking up and setting boundaries impacted my boss, other employees, and me because I had been nice, putting up with unacceptable behavior to keep the peace in the name of trying to help someone. It could have cost me my job. I needed to make some changes now.

STANDING MY GROUND

As I continued to develop my intuition, Doug also trusted it and even began to rely on it. A few months after Kit was let go, I was sitting in a meeting with Doug and the financial controller. Doug requested work to be completed in a certain way. I don't recall what the specific topic was, but I do recall what transpired. I asked a couple of questions. Then I alluded to the fact that there was a more effective way to proceed with the work and communication. Before I realized what I was doing, my hands were in the air in front of me, cupping around an imaginary ball. Then I moved my right hand up over the ball and back and forth a couple of times across the top, as if I were a fortune teller receiving a message from a crystal ball. I blurted out, "I see in my crystal ball," and told him the outcome I predicted, which wasn't favorable if we communicated the way he suggested.

He slightly raised one eyebrow, probably thinking I was a little strange. Understandably, he asked us to proceed as he had requested, and we did. Within a week or two, what I had predicted came true. At the next meeting, the exact same thing happened, and what I predicted once again came true within a week. This was the beginning of Doug learning to trust my intuition.

That fall, along with Doug, I attended a family office conference in Chicago, where family members and executives from family offices all over the world met. One thing I learned was that the family office environment brings out strange behaviors in people. I was happy to have that confirmation from other executives who experienced similar situations at their family offices. In addition to dealing with an employee doing drugs on the job, some of the other employee behaviors I dealt with included stealing, poor decision-making that financially impacted the family, the inability to manage emotions, crazy beliefs about money, an entitlement attitude, and poor personal hygiene habits. Setting clear expectations and boundaries and having difficult conversations were necessary for each of these situations, which pushed me to grow to be a more effective leader.

One of the most challenging situations I faced four years after Kit was let go was dealing with one of Doug's long-time friends, who was also a paid consultant. I had a strong inkling that he was doing something shady. Although I had that strong, knowing feeling, I couldn't pinpoint any one thing right away. But just a couple of months later, I noticed some expenses charged to a work credit card that weren't related to the family office. I knew the consultant, Les, also consulted for other companies, and maybe the transactions belonged to them.

I asked the controller to look into the transactions. She responded oddly. Her shoulders drew in, and I could see her body jittering. She hurried into her office and came right back out and whispered, "Shhhhhh. Don't say anything to anyone." Then she turned and hurried back into her office. Although she was a very levelheaded person, she seemed somewhat uncomfortable with checking into the transactions. I knew she was quite conflict-averse because at lunch a couple of times, she had shared a story about a scuffle breaking out on the football field while she watched NFL games with her dad on Sundays. She had said she'd had to go to the bathroom when that happened, and she couldn't come out for several minutes until she knew the pushing and shouting were over.

During the previous Sunday's football game, several scuffles had broken out. She had chuckled as she told us over lunch break that she'd had to go to the bathroom a lot that day.

Understanding that, I also realized why the controller was uncomfortable looking into the transactions. She was friends with Les and likely felt uneasy that I was inquiring about his purchases. The only problem was that it was part of her job. A few months later, she ended up leaving the family office before the situation resolved, but the transactions continued.

I wanted to approach Doug to let him know something was off, but I needed to figure out how to say it. I felt an internal conflict because, on the one hand, I felt like I was betraying Les. We used to have such a close relationship that, at one point, he affectionately called me his "work wife." But my loyalties were to Doug, and I took my stewardship responsibilities seriously. It was my duty to look out for Doug, and it was my duty to tell him the good, the bad, and the ugly, no matter if I wanted to or not. I just wasn't exactly sure how to approach Doug, since he and Les had been friends for nearly twenty years and Doug had been employing him for at least fifteen of those years. I knew Doug would have to grapple with his emotions stirred by the possibility of a friend betraying him and the relationship changing. But I also didn't have enough facts gathered to prove anything. I was still going off my feeling, which at that point had intensified tremendously. The knowing sense I had was only an opening point to the conversation I would have with Doug. By this time, he very much trusted my intuition, but I also knew I would need to substantiate my knowing feeling with facts.

During our meeting, Doug and I agreed I would request reports from the staff accountant and ask him to keep my requests confidential. After scouring through reports, I uncovered a pattern of transactions charged to the family office credit card that indeed were not family office expenses. The charges were substantial.

Doug talked with Les and requested he provide additional details to support all his credit card purchases. After that conversation, Les started treating me differently and talked behind my back to my employees, which created an uncomfortable rift in the small office. During one of our confrontations, Les told me to my face that I used to be a great manager and had built an excellent team, but since I started doing my personal work I had become an angry person. Further, he insisted that all my employees were unhappy and looking for new jobs because I was a lousy manager. Then he said that he didn't trust me. I told him I didn't trust him either and that he was creating problems in the office. He simply needed to provide the information requested along with the receipts, and I wouldn't have an issue.

After our conversation, when I stepped back to evaluate what he said to me, I knew the majority of my employees were happy and not looking for jobs. The staff accountant was more engaged than he'd ever been because of the changes we had made to his role, including more meaningful projects he enjoyed working on. The property manager was happy with the additional training, responsibilities, and increased salary he had recently received.

I also knew the "angry person" comment wasn't right because I was happier as a result of doing my work. The more I did, the freer I felt and the happier I was. The fact was, the more personal work I did, the more authentic I became, and the better manager I was. But with that, the more I could also see people blaming me for their behaviors instead of taking personal responsibility for them.

I think one of the best things about Doug was that he was doing his work too, which enabled us to have authentic conversations as we worked through some difficult situations. Doug reminded me to do my work each time he slid the phrase, "Another goddamn opportunity for personal growth," into our conversation. I laughed and took the cue to do my work. And I liked that I felt heard by Doug and that he valued my insights. He asked me to keep doing what I was doing because it was my job and the right thing, even though it was uncomfortable. Ultimately, Les made a series of poor choices including abusing substances that resulted in him not returning to the family office without Doug having to do anything to end the contract.

YOU OWE ME

Despite working through many emotions from being sexually abused, periodically another aspect would show up for me to work through that impacted my ability to speak up and say no.

After getting certified as an EFT practitioner, I rented a room at Blissful Balance, a center focused on healing and strengthening the mind, body, and spirit. In addition to my job, I coached clients on Fridays and Saturdays in groups and one-on-one sessions. One Friday, I was leading a weekly group tapping session I called a tapping circle, where people came together in person for tapping and support. The same people often returned week after week, which created a sense of community as we got to know each other.

There were five of us there that morning, all regular tapping-circle attendees who were sitting in a circle in the room. I faced the door so that I could greet anyone coming into the room. Barbara sat in a chair to the left of me. Patti, my EFT practitioner friend, sat in a chair across from me with the closed door to her back. Maureen and Donna sat to my right on the black leather two-seater couch. On this particular day, Donna once again interrupted inappropriately, asking another tapper a question as I guided them through a personal situation. Although I had previously pulled Donna aside after a tapping circle and asked her not to interrupt, she did it again anyway. I knew I needed to say something. But at that moment, I froze. My mind felt like the bubbles embedded in thick ice on a frozen lake. I knew I was in the room where I was holding the tapping circle and who was with me, but I couldn't speak. It was all in slow motion, and I just stared for a few moments. Barbara and Patti asked if I was okay. I nodded to let them know I was.

Luckily it was near the end of class, and Patti was there to help guide the tappers until I could speak again. After class, she stayed and helped me work through what had caused me to freeze instead of speaking up. Suddenly a dreaded memory popped into my mind.

It was dusk and time for me to leave after hanging out with Dan's sister for several hours after school. *Oh good,* I thought as I looked at the clock. *I will make it back home just in time to meet my curfew.* My mom was a stickler about arriving home on time. If I was late, it often resulted in me being grounded. I said goodbye to my friend and, as I had done so many times before, walked out the patio door onto the deck and stepped down onto their impeccably groomed green lawn. As

I continued walking through the Hurtzmans' back yard to an opening in bushes that led me to a neighboring yard, I heard a branch crackle and leaves rustling.

Oh my gosh, what's that? My heart leaped out of my chest as I looked to my left and saw Dan running right toward me. Even though I knew who he was, he scared the crap out of me, and I completely froze. I just stood there. I could feel the blood pumping through my heart as it pounded beneath my shirt, but I couldn't get my now-stiff and heavy legs to move.

Oh no, not again. What does he want this time?

As he raced closer to me, I attempted to brace myself, preparing for the impact. *Bam!* He ran into me like he was tackling his opponent on the football field and knocked my 105-pound, five-foot-two-inch body down to the ground. My butt hit the grass and dirt. It wasn't until later that I felt the sting from the scrape on my left elbow. He pinned me tight to the ground, with his muscular body firmly pushing down against mine. I could hardly breathe. One of his hands grabbed both of my wrists, and I felt each one of his fingers pushing into my skin as he tightened his grip. He quickly slid his other hand down my pants and into my underwear and inserted his cold fingers inside me. I winced in pain because it fucking hurt, and I wanted to cry.

I am so sick of this, I shouted in my mind. *Leave me alone. I have to get home.* My mind had abruptly switched from being surprised and freezing to anger and moved into fight mode. I screamed at him to stop, hoping someone would hear and come to my rescue. "Don't touch me! Get off me!" I don't know if I kneed him or kicked him, but whatever I did, I did it as hard as I could from the strange angle I was

ON THE OTHER SIDE

restrained. I knew I hit the target when his hands recoiled to protect his own body, and he groaned in pain.

I will never forget the words he uttered next. "You owe me!"

"Owe you? Owe YOU? Owe you what? I don't owe you a damn thing!" I got up off the ground as quickly as I could and started running toward home. I had no idea if he would get up and chase after me or if I had kicked him hard enough to keep him down. I just kept running. I arrived home just in time for my mom to ground me for being late. I didn't tell her why I was late. Nor did she ask. Once again, I kept the secret. I was afraid she wouldn't believe me, or that she'd think it was my fault or think I was a bad daughter and she shouldn't have adopted me. I went to my room and cried myself to sleep.

It was a big secret for a fourteen-year-old girl to keep inside, but it felt way harder for me to tell someone about what was going on. I couldn't ever make the words come out. I didn't even want to think about it—I just kept pretending it wasn't happening. And when I used my voice and stood up to him, it didn't seem to matter. He kept doing it many more times.

As that memory concluded in my mind, the words "You owe me" echoed loudly in my head. Back in the room, still tapping through the points with Patti that whole time, I angrily blurted out, "I don't owe you fucking shit, asshole! I don't owe you a damn thing. Get the fuck off of me, and don't ever touch me again."

We were both surprised at the sound of my voice, but also knew we were onto something that I needed to tap on more to fully process through the emotions and let it all go. So I set off on a tapping rant to let all my emotions out. Then I tapped focusing on the word "no," followed by a tapping argument alternating yes and no phrases. Whatever else came to mind, I let it rip while continuously tapping. I started feeling better and stronger. Just like when I was tapping on "I am worthy," the better I felt, the more I wanted my no to be stronger. That feeling fueled my fire to keep tapping.

"No, no, no, no, no, no!"

After about fifteen minutes of tapping, I shouted the word "No!" It came out more powerfully than the meek no I had uttered just a few minutes prior. I continued with more tapping and more ranting.

Every no in my voice shifted ever so slightly in a cumulative effect; at the end of the tapping, I was able to comfortably and confidently say a firm, definite NO. There was zero fear left inside my body about being hurt or retaliated against if I said no.

I felt like the tapping helped me speak up for myself and now say the things that I hadn't been able to say back then. I sat up tall in my chair, pushed my shoulders back, and happily repeated no to Patti. She smiled and nodded, acknowledging my excellent work.

Before this tapping session, I had heard the phrase "No is a complete sentence" many times before, but I'd had a hard time saying just the word no to others. Almost every time I got up the courage to say no to someone, I felt like I had to justify it with some explanation because I was afraid they would be upset with me for saying no.

If someone asked me to do something that I realized I didn't have time to help them with, then I told them the list of things I had to get done, proving there wasn't time to help them. I did that because I felt bad for saying no to them and wanted to let them down easy so they wouldn't be upset with me. Now I understood why I couldn't just say no back then. All the times I said no to Dan were ignored, and it felt like he had taken my no away from me. I'm happy I worked through that and now use *no* or *no thank you* as a complete sentence whenever I want.

Chapter Ten

CHRISTMAS IN JULY

THE COOKIE DEBACLE

In the summer of 2014, my oldest brother John and his wife and young son flew to Minnesota for a visit. We all gathered in my other brother Joe's house, planning to celebrate my nephew's second birthday, ooh and aah over the fireworks at the park on the Fourth of July, and decorate Christmas cookies.

Decorating Christmas cookies in July was not the norm for us, but it had been several years since all three of us siblings were together for December. So I figured, why not decorate Christmas cookies in July for fun? The others might have thought I was a little crazy, but they agreed to do it.

When we were kids, my mom would make the dough, roll it out thin, and use special metal cookie cutters to cut Christmas-themed cookies. Then she would mix up at least five different colors of frosting for us to use on the cookies. We would get creative and transform a snowman into a set of tired-looking eyeballs and frost the tree cookies nontraditional colors. My mom preferred that we didn't eat our artistic creations. Instead, she would create individual cookies for us that she called *blobs*. She would form them with the dough scraps, and we would each decorate a blob with as much frosting and toppings as we wanted. But after eating our blobs and decorating a few plates of cookies, the novelty would begin to fade. By the time we'd get down to the last plate of cookies, we'd quickly move through the assembly line with little to no originality. After all the cookie decorating was complete, the cookies would get tucked away in a cookie box to later be added to yummy-looking cookie plates as gifts for special family and friends. I always felt proud seeing our colorful cookies displayed on a platter at my grandparents' house at Christmastime.

But after my brother Joe and his wife Denise moved into their new home, Denise excitedly took over the cookie-baking process. She loved to bake and had a large kitchen with plenty of counter space on the island that made it extra-easy to make them. Plus, they had a dining table that expanded with extra table leaves as our families grew with their three boys and my son.

That July, we gathered at Joe and Denise's home. In the kitchen, Denise prepared the different-colored frosting bowls while I set the plates, spoons, butter knives, and a variety of multicolored toppings on the large dining table. Joe brought up additional chairs from the basement while John sat on the steps chatting with us. Joe's three teenage sons entertained their young cousin, along with John's wife. We were all there except for my mom. She was late again, and she didn't call, text, or send a carrier pigeon with a message to communicate with us.

Denise didn't like it when people arrived late to an event she hosted. She felt it was disrespectful. And my mom had been late many times since Joe and Denise first started dating. So when my mom arrived, she was greeted with an echoing "Hi, Mom" from John, Joe, and me; but as Denise stretched across the table to put a bowl of red frosting down, she sarcastically said, "Nice of you to show up on time."

Mom, taken by surprise, snipped back, "Well. I didn't know we started at a specific time. You didn't communicate clearly." "I texted you 2:00 to 5:00 p.m. That's pretty clear," Denise retorted. That set a string of snippy comments in motion back and forth across the table between the two of them. Then my mom got up from behind the table and walked toward the kitchen with comments still flying between her and Denise.

Oh my God, this isn't good, I thought. *They just aren't understanding each other. Maybe I can help.* I stepped in between the two of them. I wanted to provide some clarity. "Mom, what she means is—"

But before I could finish, Mom reacted by raising her voice louder, and I stepped back out of the way. She yelled to Denise, "You're not part of the family."

Denise looked shocked. Then she screamed back, "What the hell are you talking about? I've been in this family for twenty-five years. You don't think I am a part of it?"

All my nephews went downstairs, and John's wife followed. John stayed in the room, sitting on the steps with his arms crossed and a displeased scowl on his face. Denise's face was red, and she was crying as she stomped out of the house. The door slammed behind her. This was the first time I'd seen her leave her home during a family feud.

After Joe watched his wife leave their home, he then turned to our mom with a stern look on his face, raised his voice, and said to her, "You need to leave."

Our five-foot-tall mother looked up at my five-foot-ten brother and in a quiet and disempowered voice said to him, "Can't you see? I'm the victim here."

Before I could stop it, I busted out laughing. It was too strange to see my mom talking to my brother as though she

135

were a wronged child. But I knew right away my laughter would only make the situation worse. I slapped my hand to my mouth. Then I slid open the patio door, stepped out onto the deck, and closed the door behind me.

Oh my God, that's ridiculous. She's not a fucking victim, I thought, and my mind flashed to previous conversations where my mom and I had talked about not playing the victim. I didn't see my mom as a victim when I was a kid or as an adult. I saw her working hard to raise three kids the best she could, and we all turned out to be responsible adults who she was quite proud of. It was an old story, and I was weary of hearing it.

I stepped back inside in time to hear Joe ask our mom to leave again. She grimaced, put her head down, and proceeded to gather her items and head to the door. After my mom left, my oldest brother John stood up on the steps and looked over at me with his eyes flashing like angry daggers.

"I can't believe how you acted just now," he yelled sternly. "You were completely out of line!"

I was surprised. He had been quiet during the whole argument, but now he was yelling at me angrily. According to him, I was the problem.

"What are you talking about?" I shouted back, suddenly angry. "Why are you blaming me? I am not responsible for all of this."

"You stepped in. Every time the fight was dying down, you had to say something. You made it worse. Denise may have started it, but you kept it going. You are mean!"

I was surprised. I had stepped between my mom and Denise to try to calm things down, yet my brother thought I made it worse and that I was mean. I couldn't understand how I might have escalated the situation. So I lashed back at him.

"I stepped in to help them understand each other. My laughing didn't help the situation. So I went outside. You don't live here. You don't see all the stuff that's been going on for years between them. I am not taking the blame for this."

We were both very upset. It was clear to me that he had already decided I was wrong. He didn't want to hear it. I knew yelling at each other wouldn't solve anything. I wanted time to myself to breathe and sort this out. After a few uncomfortable minutes of silence, I said I thought it was best if I left. I said goodbye to them and whomever else had resurfaced from the basement, and then I left.

Over the next day or two, I didn't join in the family gatherings. I was hurt and upset. But this gave me space and time to step back to look at the situation. I was able to reflect on my actions.

I realized my brother was right: I had behaved ridiculously butting into their fight, inappropriately laughing, and raising my voice.

Reflecting on that day, I also realized that our family carried a lot of unacknowledged pain. This event wasn't unusual, after all. I saw how, over the years, we had somehow become accustomed to this type of carrying-on at family gatherings as if it were normal. In fact, it had become a regular occurrence to have raised voices, especially on birthdays and holidays. I remembered there was once a blowout over a misunderstanding my divorced parents had about some photos from thirty or forty years earlier at my nephew's fifteenth birthday party. And a few years before that, when traveling to a family wedding, we had a verbal altercation on the street down by the pier in San Francisco and again on a trolley car. So it was far from the first time we had misbehaved together. But John hadn't experienced any of that craziness because he was removed from most of the family gatherings by way of proximity.

He doesn't understand, I thought. *He never has to deal with Mom during moments like these. He inserts himself when he wants, defending her and making the rest of us out to be the bad guys.*

But seeing John react so strongly to my actions set me on a quest. I wasn't ready to apologize to anyone, but I wanted to figure out why I had laughed at my mom and if my actions came from some kind of mean intention, like my brother said. That meant I had to take a good look at my behaviors and be honest with myself.

RECLAIM, OWN, AND INTEGRATE

At the same time, I was already a few weeks into Nancy Levin's coaching program. I had heard Nancy speak onstage at Hay House's I Can Do It seminar the previous month. There was something in her story that had resonated with me so much that I had purchased her book and read it cover to cover on the flight home. When I arrived home, I immediately signed up for her Jump Group Coaching program.

Before our next coaching call, I posted in the private Jump Facebook group the story about laughing at my mom during a family feud. I felt vulnerable about sharing my embarrassing behavior, but my desire to change was greater, and I felt safe seeking help from the group. Nancy commented on my post, "Thank you for your open, honest, and raw share. Here goes . . . "

Oh no, I thought worriedly. *What is she going to say?* I gulped and continued reading.

"This all points back," Nancy went on, "to reclaiming and owning and integrating the disowned parts of ourselves, the parts we absolutely don't want to be—judgmental and mean for starters. We are everything. Your relationship with your mother, and each member of your family, will change as you live by example. It's not about them. And it's not only about change. It's about living and relating with integrity honoring authentic truth. It's about you setting a clear boundary and holding true to it. It will be a pattern interrupt. There's no one to please anymore. No one to seek approval from. No one to give you permissions. Just you."

At first, I didn't understand what the heck she was saying, so I read it a few times to allow it to soak in. I eventually realized it to mean that it's really about loving and accepting all of ourselves: the good, the bad, the ugly—all of it.

As I thought back on the cookie-decorating debacle and how I could have behaved differently, I first had to own my judgment, mainly against my mom for claiming she was a victim. In a one-on-one coaching session with Nancy, we took a look at why the word *victim* triggered me and caused me to laugh inappropriately.

Nancy guided me to close my eyes and go within my heart. The belief I discovered I held was that being a victim is weak. I didn't want to be a victim because I had been one in my childhood. It was disempowering. I wanted to do whatever I could to not be a victim ever again. With that awareness, Nancy guided me to reclaim, own, and integrate the disowned-victim part of me. I took a deep breath in, let it out, and said the words I heard from my heart: "I have been a victim. It's part of my life. It's part of my story."

I paused for a moment and then let out a sigh. "But I don't have to stay a victim."

I quietly sat with that. Then I felt tears pool up behind my eyes as I thought about my mom. I felt my heart flutter and thought, *Oh, Mom, I love you.*

"I don't see my mom as a victim," I told Nancy. "She's strong and has been through so much in life. I suppose that's why I laughed. But I can see why she thinks she is a victim, and I can love her right where she is at, even if I don't like it or agree with her."

I saw the whole cookie debacle from a different standpoint. I could see how both Denise and my mom felt attacked and went into fight-flight-freeze mode. They had yelled at each other to protect themselves. They both had reacted naturally, and so had I.

EVERY SINGLE TIME

Just a month after the cookie debacle, I participated in a five-day Ultimate You Retreat in the Twin Cities led by Dr. Paul Scheele. Paul is a spiritual teacher and coach who guides people to start using the innate resources we all have within our subconscious minds. There were about twenty participants that flew in from all over the US, and one guy even flew in from the UK. We were together for twelve hours a day, learning about different spiritual practices, experimenting with intuition, and tuning in to our powerful minds.

I observed Paul for clues about handling stressful situations. I saw how loving and kind he was with one participant, a man named Gary, who was having trouble understanding the lessons. Paul was patient with him, especially when others were frustrated with him.

I didn't get it.

How can he be so patient and so kind to this guy when he just doesn't have a clue? I wondered. *How is Paul not getting worked up with him for being so stupid and not taking personal responsibility for his life?*

I didn't understand how he could be so loving and kind to somebody who wasn't clicking with the group, who wasn't open and paying attention. I was so confused. I knew those thoughts weren't okay to say out loud. I felt like I was supposed to be more loving and compassionate than how I was thinking.

I noticed that I avoided interacting with Gary altogether. I felt uncomfortable around him. I didn't know what to say to him. Everyone else had already said all the same things I would have said. I wanted to learn how to deal with this situation in a different way.

This was "another goddamn opportunity for personal growth," as Doug would say; and it was a safe space for me to explore how to deal with it. On the last night, I sat at the dinner table with Paul and two other attendees. I told Paul how all week long I'd been observing everyone interact with Gary. I saw others trying to coach him and help him, even though he wasn't able to listen or hear them. I saw the resistance. I saw them give up in frustration. Yet every time Paul interacted with Gary, he was so loving and kind. I asked him how he did that because I wanted to know how to be that way.

Then I told him the story of when I laughed at my mom

and my brother called me mean, and how I didn't feel good about any of it. I didn't want to be that way. Feeling desperate, I asked, "How do I change, Paul? How do I become more patient with people who frustrate me?"

Paul said, "Whatever your reaction is, is about you, Julie. It's not about the other person. You need to do your own personal work to heal it."

I wanted to clarify to make sure I understood what he said. "So you're saying that whenever I am triggered, no matter what they did or said, when I am upset or any other negative emotion, I have to do my own personal work? Every single time?"

"Yes, Julie, that's exactly right," Paul confirmed. "You can only control you. When you are triggered, you need to do your work. Keep doing your work. The more you do it, the more you'll understand it's not about the other person. It's about cleaning your side of the street. You can't just sweep it once. You have to sweep it regularly."

"I've heard that message before," I said. "But what about the other person? Isn't it ever their fault? Is this true across the board every single time?"

Paul nodded as he replied, "Yes, Julie, this applies every single time. Keep doing your work."

I sat with that new understanding, feeling it hit me like an open-handed slap on the face. I'd been impatient and mean to my mom for a very long time. I was judging the hell out of her for thoughts I made up in my head about how she should behave.

Especially when I was a teen, I had never felt understood by my mom. I didn't feel like I could share anything personal with her own firm beliefs. I didn't feel like I could ask her questions about God if I didn't understand because I was just supposed to believe, and she rarely got my sense of humor. I imagine she felt misunderstood by me as well. I had to let that old story go and find ways to love and appreciate my mom for who she was, not who I thought she should be. I knew I had to change myself because I couldn't change her no matter how hard I tried.

I also couldn't control if she did her personal work or not. I needed to focus on me and my work and let go of any expectations that she do hers. The word *expectation* sounded louder in my head than the other words.

I remembered a phrase Doug had said a few times: "Expectations are premeditated resentments." That made me stop to take a closer look at what else I expected of my mom. Surprisingly, I had quite a list. I had heard people say so often, "When you're older, you're wiser." Simply because my mom was older than I was, I expected her to be further along on her spiritual journey than me. I thought she should have been the one who taught me these spiritual lessons when I was a kid instead of me learning from others as an adult. And I had expected her to be able to communicate way better than me.

I had silently placed a whole bunch of expectations on my mom; and when she didn't meet them, I resented her, looked down on her, judged her, and was mean to her.

When I saw my behaviors in those snapshots, I saw the truth: I often wasn't kind to my mother. There were many times that I was rude to her on holidays because she didn't do things the way that I had expected, or she was late to a gathering. I treated her poorly when she didn't live up to my expectations.

It was painful to see and admit to myself how unfair I had been. Yes, I had been mean. But at least now I understood why.

BREAKING THE SILENCE

While I tried to figure out how to make up for my mistake, I recalled a story that Cindy, another mindset coach I had worked with, had shared with me about how she had struggled with her mom. She had realized her mom's health was digressing rapidly and wanted to be loving and kind to her. She wanted to enjoy the little amount of remaining time they had together. She told me she used to put together music playlists of different songs from her mom's high school days. Listening to those songs uplifted her mom, made her feel good, and positively impacted her mood.

Cindy also made sure not to bring up any past unresolved conflicts from her teen years and didn't pick fights with her mom, because none of it mattered. She couldn't change her mom, so she changed herself and focused on being in the present moment to enjoy the time with her mom.

After she had shared that with me, a lightbulb went off in my head. I saw how I could significantly impact my relationship with my mom for the better by choosing in advance how I want to be and feel when I'm with her. Although my mom's health wasn't digressing rapidly due to illness and I wasn't expecting her to die anytime soon, she was in her early seventies and showing some physical signs of aging. I wanted to take a lesson from friends who had lost their parents and had regrets of not having a better relationship with them before they passed. I didn't want to have regrets but wanted to be more intentional, like my mindset coach was with her mom. I wanted to connect with my mom now so we could enjoy our relationship and I could have good memories with her. I wanted to leave behind all the past crap and be present every time I was with her. That was a new way of thinking and being for me, letting the past go and being present with her. I was wise enough to know I couldn't change overnight but promised myself I would keep working on it.

I could start the shift by apologizing to her.

My mom and I still hadn't talked since that fight at my brother's house five weeks prior, so I called her and asked if I could stop by her house. Luckily, she was open to it. When I drove to her house, I bawled almost the whole way because I felt so bad for all the times I had treated her poorly. I tried to compose myself before I arrived at her house. I pulled up into her driveway, took a deep breath in, and slowly walked down the fourteen long cement steps to her home.

I saw her outside on the patio with her small white Maltese puppies, Benji and Bella. I walked over to her.

We greeted each other uncomfortably with a strained hello. We didn't hug. We sat inside the screened tent she had set up in her back yard with a white plastic table and two matching chairs. Finally, I broke the uneasy silence by telling her about the retreat I had just returned from.

"I experienced a few things that I think you'd like to hear about," I told her.

"Oh, what did you do at the retreat?" she inquired as she leaned toward me with interest. The icy silence seemed to disappear.

"We did all sorts of things," I said excitedly. "We started

each morning with yoga and meditation. Many days, the guy running the retreat led us through an activity that helped us become more aware of personal habits and behaviors. One of the days, I had an interesting connection about why I eat so much ice cream."

"Oh, I'd like to hear that. I know you like ice cream. I do too."

"When I am stressed out," I explained, "I crave ice cream so I can feel better. I think my subconscious mind associates ice cream with happiness because Grandpa used to treat me to ice cream cones when I would stay with him and Grandma. My subconscious mind is trying to help me feel better when I am stressed out. And now that I know that, I can enjoy eating ice cream when I crave it instead of thinking I shouldn't be eating it and beating myself up afterward."

She nodded in interest, and we chatted about it a bit longer, discussing our shared cravings for ice cream. But after a while, I reluctantly switched the subject.

"Mom, I realized another thing during the retreat. When we were at Joe's for cookie-decorating and I laughed during the argument, that was probably really hurtful to you."

I took a deep breath in and slowly continued. "I've been hurtful to you many times over the years. I just didn't realize I was doing it at the time." I pushed back the tears that were on the verge of spilling out. "Mom, I am so sorry for being unkind to you. Will you ever forgive me?"

She nodded and accepted my apology, to my relief. And although we both shifted in that moment, we felt a little leery about how to move forward. We still had other bad memories of hurtful times from the past. But we agreed we would take things slowly as we rebuilt our trust with each other.

Over time, I continued to take responsibility for my

reactions and do my personal work. I found that I presented my best self to my mom when I followed my own boundaries. I still followed my 9:00 p.m. curfew, but I also let her know when I was unable to talk if I wasn't in a good space to listen well. It wasn't unkind to say no to talking on the phone to take care of myself. It made our interactions better when I didn't talk on the phone at times when I had a short fuse because of something else I was working through in my life. I didn't want that to spill over onto my mom. Instead, I would text her photos of me so she could feel connected. Because that was what she was looking for: connection. That's what we all are looking for from others, especially from the people we love.

Chapter Eleven

FORGIVENESS IS A PROCESS

HURT PEOPLE HURT PEOPLE

A few months after I had apologized to my mom about being unkind, I had another coaching session with Cindy. This time, it was on forgiveness.

When she used "forgive" and "abuser" in the same sentence in a suggestive manner to me, I thought, *No fucking way! No fucking way am I going to forgive the person who abused me. What he did was WRONG. How could I forgive him for what he did? I don't want to forgive him!*

It was probably good that she couldn't see my eyes popping open wide in disbelief over the phone, but I'm sure she felt my discord in how I responded "What?" with a you-are-fucking-crazy tone.

"Julie, hurt people hurt people. When people are hurt, they lash out and hurt other people—sometimes consciously, and other times they have no idea they are even doing it. Since he was hurting you, it's likely someone was hurting him, because what he did to you is not normal behavior. What he did to you comes from a hurt person."

Up until that moment, I had never thought *he* was abused or hurt by someone and therefore abusing me. I understood the phrase "hurt people hurt people." However, my deeper understanding didn't ease any of my pain or make me want to forgive him. I still wasn't ready to forgive him.

How could I? I thought. *What he did was wrong! Forgiving him would let him off the hook.*

As I struggled with these thoughts of forgiveness, the experience of my birth mother and birth father came into my mind. By that time in my life, I had met both of my birth parents.

I had first contacted my birth mother seventeen years earlier, just before my son was born, and then contacted my birth father five years later. My birth parents were two young adults when they fell in love; they got engaged when she was nineteen and he was twenty-three. I imagined how much fun they must have had when they had conceived me out of wedlock. They were flirting with each other, got a little "hot and heavy" on the couch. Next thing you know, they were making love—and *bam*! In that moment of excitement, joy, and ecstasy, I was conceived. At least that's what I liked to pretend. It helped me believe it was a happy time for them at that moment, even though I later found out it wasn't a happy time when my birth mother first learned she was pregnant with me.

We had reconnected over the phone when I was twenty-six. My birth mother told me she always knew I would contact her someday, and she felt excited about it. But I could sense by the tone of her voice that she also had a lot of pent-up feelings about my birth father, from all that she had gone through. As she told me the story of my birth, I could tell anger was the primary emotion she aimed toward him.

Clearly, I wasn't planned. After my birth mother told my birth father she was pregnant, she never saw or heard from him again. I can't imagine how she must have felt. Back in the late 1960s and early '70s, if a young lady got pregnant out of wedlock, it was highly frowned upon. Society viewed it as an embarrassment to the family and downright shameful. My birth mother had to leave her home and move out of town while she was pregnant. Fortunately, her aunt and uncle took her in and supported her until she gave birth. Her younger siblings had no idea she was pregnant and were under the impression she had gone off to college. Her pregnancy and childbirth were well-kept secrets, not to be talked about for a very long time.

When it was time for her to head to the hospital, her mother met her there. Within forty-eight hours, she gave birth to me, held me, and gave me up for adoption. Many times I've thought of the strength and courage it must have taken for her to have me and give me up, as well as the array of emotions she likely had mixed up inside her during that time.

As we slowly got to know each other over several years and spent a small amount of time together in person, she shared some of her life stories with me, and I could see the anger had impacted her mind and body. I could also hear the argument going on inside her mind about building a relationship with me. On the one hand, we had some cool things in common, and I could tell she liked me. But on the other hand, I was a big, sore reminder of *him*.

It didn't seem to me that she had any intention of processing emotions or letting go of that part of her life. She was doing her best to keep it stuffed down because it hurt when it came up. It was emotional for me when I realized our relationship likely wouldn't develop any further because of the pain those memories brought her. At the same time that I felt sadness for myself over the loss of what could have been, I felt sorrow for her that she still felt angry after all those years.

My birth parents hadn't seen or talked to each other in over thirty years by the time I met my birth father, and he was unaware my birth mother was angry with him. Her anger wasn't impacting him—it was only impacting her like a poisonous drink.

Thinking about my birth parents helped me understand that I needed to forgive my abuser. The very thing I saw her struggle with, I was doing to myself. But like her, I wasn't quite ready to grapple with my past either.

Cindy's voice brought me back to the present as she gave me a homework assignment. "All right, Julie. This week, you're to write your abuser a letter. You need to find compassion for him and forgive him because undoubtedly he was hurting to do that to you. Then you need to wish him all the things you'd like for yourself, like feeling safe, having amazing relationships, and feeling peace inside. That's your homework. Any questions?"

I was still in disbelief. I was the one who had been abused by him, and yet she wanted me to find compassion for *him*. Forgive *him*. Wish good things for *him*. "Uh. Do I have to do this? I don't want to write *him* a letter."

"You don't need to mail it to him," she said. "You need to write it out so you can forgive him and free yourself from the pain you're in. Be sure to let me know when you're done." My homework assignments were always due at least twenty-four hours before our next call. Since I had time that night and the following day, I figured I might as well get started instead of dreading it all week long.

DEAR DAN

I felt a lot of resistance inside because I didn't want to do the assignment. But Cindy's job was to push me out of my comfort zone. That's what I was paying her to do. I remembered a mantra I had learned years earlier from Tony Robbins: "If you can't, you must." So I begrudgingly started writing.

Even though I knew I wouldn't send him the letter, it wasn't easy to write to someone I hadn't talked to (nor wanted to talk to) in years. It felt awkward and uncomfortable, trying to figure out what I wanted to express. I didn't know how to start the letter, but eventually I started writing and referred back to my notes in my coaching journal to get an idea of what I could write next. I did what she guided me to do, but frankly I just wanted to get it over and done with and slam the door shut on that part of my life.

Dear Dan,

We haven't seen each other or talked in years, so this letter may be somewhat out of the blue.

I'm contacting you to release you from all this crap I've been carrying around all of these years and to forgive you.

Your behaviors to me physically caused me a lot of harm that I've spent a lot of time dealing with so I could resolve it and move on. Specifically I've had issues with men where I haven't felt safe or haven't been able to trust them. I didn't realize how all this was tied together and remained tied together because I hadn't let go, forgiven you, or released you.

I'm ready to do that now. I'm ready to tell you that I understand your behaviors and the way you treated me were not normal behaviors. I don't know what you were going through in your life at that time to cause you to touch me the way you touched me and to restrain me and hurt me.

Dan, that was so hard on me. I had bumps and bruises and cuts. I was hurt physically and emotionally. I was confused. I don't know if all those things I experienced were being done to you, too, or what was going on in your world. But today is the day that I cut our connecting cord. Today is the day I release you. Today is the day I forgive you. Today is the day I let go and move into my new life.

Daniel Hurtzman, I forgive you. May you heal. May you love fully. May you feel safe and make others feel safe around you. May you have the most amazing relationships. May your days be filled with love, peace, joy, compassion, grace, and understanding.

—Julie

That seemed like a valiant effort, but looking back at the letter now, I understand I didn't lean in and truly feel the array of emotions or the pain of the experiences because I didn't know how. The letter felt contrived and inarticulate because that's precisely where I was at that moment on my healing journey. I was going through the motions, writing what my coach told me to write. I was doing what I thought I was sup-posed to do, which in hindsight makes so much sense. I had cut off my feelings so long ago back when I was being abused, and I *had* just been going through the motions, doing what I thought I was supposed to do in all areas of my life: my marriage, my job, my family, and my home. And I didn't forgive him when I wrote that letter. It was more of a faux forgiveness. I wanted to forgive because it was the right thing to do, but I put the least amount of effort into it as possible. It was kind of like when my mom used to force me and my brother to apologize to each other when we were younger.

Joe and I were just a year apart in age and would periodically squabble as young children. My mom would force us to apologize to each other on the spot and forgive each other without talking it through or hearing each other's sides of the fight. As an adult, I understand she was trying to instill in us the act of forgiveness. But as a kid, it felt strained, forced, and uncomfortable. I offered Joe the flimsiest apology possible whenever I was still angry or hurt. And so did he.

That's what this letter felt like to me: flimsy, because I wasn't ready to forgive him.

After I finished the letter, it felt way too personal to share with my coach. Not to mention I had half-assed the assignment and didn't want her to make me write the letter over again. I sent an email to let her know I'd done my homework. She never brought it up again, nor did I. I was off the hook—because I let myself off the hook. But my healing from sexual abuse was far from over.

In fact, it had only just begun.

155

LETTING GO

Two years later, after I had completed numerous intense therapy sessions, cried an abundance of tears, tapped more sessions than I can count, and experienced countless aha moments, I was ready to forgive him genuinely. Not because someone told me to, and not because that's what I was supposed to do, but because I wanted to let go and was ready to do it. That's when the opportunity to forgive serendipitously presented itself.

Back in my room at Blissful Balance, I was placing chairs in a circle and positioning my tapping postcards on the table for any newcomers who might show up for my Friday women's tapping circle. That's when a bright yellow image of the sun on a sheet of white paper caught my eye. I picked it up and looked at it. It was a one-page flyer promoting a weekend forgiveness workshop that started that very evening and continued through late Sunday afternoon.

After the group session was over, I picked up my phone, searched for the lady's name on the flyer, and found her website. Her name and image looked familiar to me, and I recalled that we were friends on Facebook. I read her bio, which stated she had been teaching forgiveness workshops for over twenty-five years. I excitedly dialed the number listed on the flyer. I was hoping she'd answer the phone and have a seat for me. I felt a little disappointed when she didn't answer, but I left a message and my phone number.

After my next client left, I picked up my phone and noticed a voicemail message notification on the screen. I touched "Play" and listened to a friendly voice say, "Hi, Julie. This is Mary returning your call. Yes, we just had a cancellation, so there is space for you at the workshop this weekend. See you tonight at seven o'clock."

For a split second, the voice in my head wondered what I was getting into, and I thought about not attending the workshop. I quickly realized my mind was trying to protect me and talk me out of attending, just like it had wanted to protect me way back then by minimizing, ignoring, and blocking out the pain. But the words "See you tonight at seven o'clock" lingered in my mind. I felt like that flyer had been placed there for me. It wasn't just a coincidence that the flyer was in my room, that my weekend was open, and that she had space for me. I knew I needed to be there, and I knew exactly who I was going to forgive.

I contacted my Saturday client to reschedule our session. Then I put the room back in order, drove home, took a short nap, ate dinner, and drove to the historic brick-and-stone Carondelet Center in Saint Paul for the opening evening of the workshop.

As we gathered in a circle on comfy chairs and couches, the facilitator, Mary Hayes Grieco, introduced herself to us and shared the weekend's agenda. I felt a mixture of excitement and nervousness, but I knew I was in good company and that Mary was creating a safe space for us to go through this process together.

The group was a mix of thirteen women and one man who had all come together with the common desire to forgive someone. As participants briefly shared their stories, it was evident everyone was in a different place on their journey. Some people were still very angry with the person they wanted to forgive. I could tell by the inflection in their voices and the split-second grimace as they said who it was without even sharing their name. Some people were smack-dab in the middle of their divorce process, but the longing in their eyes showed they wanted to forgive their spouse. Others had been divorced a while but hadn't been able to move on entirely. Still others had come to forgive a parent who had transitioned. A few, like me, had come to forgive their abusers, including one brave young lady who was raped just a couple of weeks prior. She attended the workshop to forgive her rapist at the encouragement of her grandmother.

Wowza, I thought. *She is courageous and brave to forgive someone who just raped her a couple of weeks ago. I don't know that I could do what she's doing.*

After listening to a few people share who they were forgiving and why, it was my turn. I leaned forward in the armchair. "I am Julie. I've come here to forgive the person who sexually abused me between the ages of eleven and seventeen. I've done a shit-ton of therapy to get myself to the point where I want to forgive him for real. I understand the toll of not dealing with this had on my life, and this feels like the next right step for me to take my power back."

I could hear gasps just like when I had shared my one true sentence in the Personal Story Power workshop eighteen months before. One lady even said, "Wow, Julie, you're inspiring."

Mary explained to us that the old model for forgiveness, "forgive and forget," was quite ineffective because often people harbored resentment and other emotions inside instead of truly letting go. Those feelings didn't allow for the unconditional love to flow, which is what happens after genuinely forgiving someone. The new model of forgiveness is something that heals because it's done intentionally and helps release emotions and expectations that aren't helpful to keep inside. It's an eight-step release process.

She walked us through each step:

Step One: *Set your intention to forgive the person.*

Step Two: *Express your feelings exactly as they are inside you.*

Step Three: *Release expectations of the other person.*

Step Four: *Restore your boundaries.*

Step Five: *Open up to the Universe to get your needs met in a different way.*

Step Six: *Receive Spirit's healing energy.*

Step Seven: *Send unconditional love.*

Step Eight: *See the good in the person or situation.*

She told us that when we go through the eight steps in the new model, we would feel a peacefulness inside, but we had to decide to do it first. She also explained that when we forgive someone, we aren't condoning their behavior, taking responsibility for their actions, or letting them off the hook. We are freeing ourselves when we forgive.

The short evening felt like a perfect amount of time to ease into the forgiveness process that we would embark on the next day. Mary told us that Saturday would be a big day, and with a quick raise of her eyebrows gave us a hint she would ask for a volunteer to demonstrate the forgiveness process with her in front of the group. Out of the corner of my eye, I saw one lady's eyes widening as if she were afraid. I saw another lady fidget in her seat, then quickly look down to the floor as if she were already avoiding being called on. Although I imagined it would be tough to go through the process in front of the group, I wanted to volunteer. I knew that with Mary leading me, I would dig a lot deeper and do the work if I were doing it in front of the group. If I did it on my own during the group exercise, I might let myself off the hook again, like I had when Cindy had been my coach.

The next day, when we returned from lunch break, I didn't want to let go of this opportunity to heal, so I committed to myself to dig deep and play full-out, no matter what. We started with a meditation that helped us get grounded and connected into our hearts. At the end of the meditation, with our eyes still closed, Mary kept her word and asked for a volunteer to demonstrate the process with her at the front of the room. I raised my hand straight up in the air, which felt a lot easier to do with my eyes closed.

With my eyes closed and my hand raised, I asked God to guide me. "Please, God, if I'm selected, help me to be fully open, and please help me clear all this out and fully let go. If I'm selected, God, please let me be filled with courage so I may be a positive example for the others who will do this process after me. Thank you, God!"

After what seemed like several minutes, Mary said, "You may open your eyes." Then, in a joyful tone without skipping a beat, she said, "The lucky winner is you, Julie." She looked me in the eyes, smiled softly, and nodded like she was letting me know, *"You got this."*

I took the seat in a chair at the front of the room next to Mary and noticed an empty chair out in front of me. Mary explained to the group why the extra chair was in front of me: because I would use the Gestalt therapy empty-chair technique during the forgiveness process.

"Julie will imagine her abuser is sitting in the empty chair and speak to him throughout the forgiveness process to help her clear up unfinished business."

She further explained this technique helps us become more self-aware and helps us accept and trust our feelings and experiences that have been suppressed. I had previously tried this empty-chair technique in a different workshop and knew it worked well, so I was okay with doing it again.

Mary reminded me that I was safe, that she would guide me through the entire process, and that she would be there for me. She asked me if I was ready. I said, "Yes."

She asked me to state my intention. Tears quickly filled my eyes as I said out loud in front of the group, "I am ready to forgive my abuser, fully let go, and be free. I am ready to forgive so I can feel safe and trust men again."

I was ready to move on to Step Two and express my feelings—or so I thought.

All of a sudden, the tears that had filled my eyes were streaming down my face and flowing freely as if I had permitted them to let loose. I couldn't stop them or even hold them back. It felt miserable to feel all the emotions at once that were jumbled and bottled up from years of abuse by Dan. But I allowed myself to feel all of it. Fully.

Rage.

Anger.

Confusion.

Hurt.

Sadness.

Resentment.

Shame.

Embarrassment.

Humiliation.

In a lumpy-throated, quivering voice, I started to let it out. "I fucking hate you. You hurt me. You touched me without my permission. You were supposed to be a friend. You were supposed to be a safe male in my life."

I paused, hoping I had said enough for Mary to move on to the next step. But I knew full well that I hadn't.

Mary leaned forward and gave me a quick nod as she encouraged me to keep going. "You're doing well, Julie. Let it all out."

"You're a fuckhead. I hate you. I hate how you surprise-attacked me. I hate how you got your friends to hurt me. I hate how you were tricky. I hate all that you did to me. You're nasty and gross and mean." I was trying not to hold back, but some of it was hard to say out loud. Sometimes the sound of the words just couldn't make it past the lump in my throat, but I shouted them in my head so I could get them all out.

I was surprised at how much anger I still had inside, especially after all the hours of therapy, tapping, and healing. I thought I had dealt with all of it, but I quickly recognized the body was dutiful. Even though I worked on healing the different abuse scenes, my mind and body still concealed thoughts and emotions about *him* like I had commanded it to all those years.

With my lips pursed in anger, I told Mary, "I want to kick him in the balls and hurt him after all he did to me. It impacted my whole life! And I am angry!"

Mary grabbed a pillow off the chair, held it up against her body, and guided me. "Pretend I'm the abuser. Knee the pillow, and get all the emotions out of your body. They are buried deep within you, and you want to get them all out."

The first couple of knees to the pillow were rather wimpy

because I felt utterly stupid kneeing an offending pillow in front of the group. Besides, I was afraid I would knock Mary over. Mary obviously had seen this look of apprehension on the other brave volunteers that had role-modeled in previous workshops. So when she saw my apprehension, she encouraged me to let loose and assured me she could handle more. I reminded myself to play full-out despite feeling stupid with all eyes on me.

In my mind, I pretended she was my abuser, and he had to stand there and take it. I mustered up the courage to knee the pillow with a lot more strength.

Oh my God, did that feel good, I thought. *And Mary is pretty strong. She barely budged.*

Mary cheered me on for being brave. I straightened back up, put my hands on the front of her shoulders, and I kneed the pillow and kneed it some more.

As I kneed it, I yelled, and I cried because Dan had hurt me. I cried because I was embarrassed I was saying these things in front of the group. I cried for the younger Julie, who went through all of the abuse. I cried because I had been hurt. Then I broke down and sobbed for the younger Julie, who was sexually promiscuous with more guys than I wanted to admit to myself or anyone else.

As I sobbed, Mary cheered me on for letting out all that had been hurting me. She cheered me on for digging deep, and I could feel her love, support, and compassion for me.

I continued to sob for the younger Julie, who had an abortion just after turning sixteen years old. I couldn't summon up the strength to say that one out loud to the group between sobs and the lump in my throat. But I had shared as much as I could out loud. It was one of the most vulnerable and challenging things I had ever done—even more vulnerable than telling people I had taken money out of my son's savings account from the front of the stage with 100 people in the audience.

I kneed the pillow until I couldn't knee it anymore. All of a sudden, I just stopped and stood still. Not because I was tired or out of breath. Not because I didn't have the strength to keep kneeing. I literally couldn't do it anymore. I no longer wanted to hurt Dan, since he was a human being too.

It was like a switch shut off the desire to hurt him, and I didn't want to hurt another human being, no matter who it was or what they had done. Violent isn't who I was or who I wanted to be.

But Mary asked me to dig deep and keep going. I told her all I had left inside was the phrase on repeat that I heard replay in my head: "Shitty person, shitty person, shitty person."

Mary told us then that it's okay to feel the way I did, that what he did was shitty, no matter what. But forgiveness isn't about condoning another person's behavior. It's about getting all the old thoughts, feelings, and emotions out of our bodies and letting them go.

I said "Shitty person" a few more times, and the group began to chant in unison, "Shitty person, shitty person, shitty person." They were supporting me and letting me know that they cared about me, no matter what had happened in my past. And it was their way of encouraging me to keep going. It felt like Mary and the others in the group loved me no matter how sexually active I had been as a teen. They loved me even though I hadn't loved myself because of all the horrible things I had done as a result of being abused.

I looked up at the others watching me and quickly looked

back down at the empty chair. Though they were so supportive of me, holding space for me and encouraging me, I couldn't look at them because I was still embarrassed. It was hard enough admitting that crap out loud to myself, let alone them. Although I didn't enjoy opening up, being raw, and saying all the things in front of the group, I knew I would feel different once I got through to the other side of the process.

Then Mary explained, "The next step is to set aside your expectations of the other person. When we release expectations for people to behave in a certain way, it dissolves the attachment that blocks the flow of unconditional love to ourselves. When we open up to experiencing unconditional love for ourselves, we are able to feel the feelings of freedom, joy, and peace we long for."

When she first taught us this step, it was hard for me to understand how I would give up expectations of Dan abusing me. But as I grappled with it in my mind, I realized I did have expectations of him because I expected him *not* to abuse me. I expected him to behave in a manner that wouldn't bring harm to me. I stated out loud, "I prefer you to be a safe male, friend, and neighbor, but you weren't that. I will let go, forgive, and move on. I release the expectation that you were a safe male, friend, and neighbor." I paused and, as Mary guided me to do, I imagined all the expectations melting out of my body, leaving a clean, open space.

Then it was time to sort out and send him back his stuff, the emotional weight of him that I had carried with me all these years so that he could take on his responsibility. I no longer needed to carry those responsibilities. With my head squarely facing the chair and my eyes focused directly on the padded chair back, I stated with firm intention, "I give you full responsibility for your actions. I give you full responsibility for the laws you broke and the people you hurt."

As I said that, it felt like a huge weight lifted off my shoulders and neck. I sighed with relief. I hadn't realized how much I was carrying that wasn't even mine to carry.

With that release, we continued on to the step of opening up to the Universe to get my needs met in a new way. With Mary's guidance, I stated my intention, saying, "I'm open to being and feeling safe. I am open to feeling completely at peace."

As I said the next intention, tears streamed down my face. "I am open to loving, kind, and gentle men coming into my life, and I am open to knowing what love truly feels like from a man through experiencing it." I sat up straighter in the chair and felt my shoulders roll back and my chest expand as I allowed my heart to open up to men, who I had been so closed off to for over thirty years. I didn't know what that looked like or how the Universe would make it happen or even when. But I did know that every time I had opened myself up to trust the Universe in the past, it always conspired in my favor in ways I would have never imagined for myself.

As we continued, I didn't feel intensely raw and vulnerable as I had during other steps. Then Mary said, "It's time to send him something positive and release him. You can send him unconditional love, good luck, a strand of goodwill, love from God, or whatever you feel like you're able to send him."

After I closed my eyes, I said, "My intention is to send him unconditional love." I heard a quiet collective gasp from the group as if they were surprised that I was choosing unconditional love instead of something more comfortable, like good luck. I didn't let the gasp influence me. I knew what I wanted to send. As I imagined love coming out of my heart, floating across the air over to his heart, a single tear rolled down my right cheek; and simultaneously, a bright white light shone onto the left side of my head. For a brief moment, I was confused about what was happening. *Wait a minute,* I thought. *The sun is still shining on my right cheek. The sun goes down in the afternoon, so that's the west. The sun couldn't possibly go over the building and shine through the east window onto my left side at the same time.* More tears rolled down my cheeks, and my body felt like it had tingly amoebas floating around in sparkling golden gel. I was delighted as I realized what was happening. The bright white light was God healing me, and the amoebas were unconditional love. I felt my heart fill up and overflow with the most beautiful bursting feeling. I could hardly breathe. I sat there in silence for a moment, taking it in. I was in awe.

"Julie, the final step is to see the good in him or the good that came from the situation."

I recalled the moment in therapy the year before, when the gift from the abuse presented itself to me. I opened my eyes and shared with the group, "My gift is an uncanny and remarkable awareness of body language, including micro shifts, body movements, and facial changes." After I paused, I continued, "My keen observation of others' body movements, tone of voice, and facial expressions developed highly during the years of abuse. My mind paid extra attention to those movements to keep me safe and warn me of an impending attack. Now I see those tiny shifts and changes when talking with others and when I'm working with my clients." I paused again to allow them to take it in. "I help my clients by bringing them to their awareness." It was a gift that allowed me to help my clients have more awareness around their own thoughts and feelings. Then they could efficiently and effectively clear out old memories, feelings, and emotions that were no longer serving them.

I know this process opened me up in so many other ways, because my life changed dramatically in the following months. I finally took that big leap of faith and followed my heart to Florida after being afraid to move the previous twenty-eight years.

PART THREE

healing for the future

Chapter Twelve

THE MESSAGE IN MEDITATION

THE MESSAGE

Florida had been the secret love of my life since I was eighteen. After my first visit to Florida, I'd wanted to move there. When I graduated from high school early in January, my dad took me on my first trip to Florida as my graduation gift. I was extra-thrilled to get out of the cold and snow in Minnesota to get to be in the warm Florida sun.

When we arrived in Florida, I instantly fell in love. I loved the ocean and salty air. I loved seeing the palm trees sway in the breeze, and I loved the sunny and blue skies, especially because back home in Minnesota it was gray and dreary. I felt happy and free there.

After our planned vacation time was over, my dad headed back to Minnesota, and I got to stay for a couple more weeks with my cousins, aunt, and uncle. When it was time for me to return to Minnesota, I cried because I didn't want to leave paradise and return to the tundra. So I created a plan to move there, got accepted at the Art Institute of Fort Lauderdale, and got my scholarship approved to transfer there. I ended up not moving because I was afraid that I would go to the beach and not to class. Plus, I didn't know what I was going to be doing at the Art Institute. I liked art, but I didn't have a specific interest. The school brochures with the tantalizing images of the ocean, blue skies, and palm trees and the thought of spending more time with my cousins enticed me more than anything school-related.

But I never lost my deep desire to move to Florida.

Before Dave and I got married, I told him that I wanted three things: two kids, to travel a lot, and to move somewhere warm like Florida. After we got married, we had one kid, our traveling was limited to semi-truck shows in Kentucky (not my idea of travel), and Dave let me know he wasn't leaving Minnesota.

As Dave and I were going through our divorce, I thought about moving to Florida again and even talked with my attorney about it to make sure it was an option in our divorce decree. But I said no to myself once again because I thought my son needed to grow up near family, and it would be hard for just the two of us to move there alone.

A few years later, my new significant other and I talked about moving somewhere warm together. We took a trip to Clearwater, Florida, and once again I felt free and full of life.

I loved visiting Florida, and every time I left, I cried because I didn't want to leave. When I left California, Kauai, or other warm places, I complained that I had to go back to cold Minnesota, but I didn't cry. My soul wasn't giving up on Florida. It was knock-knock-knocking and giving me clues.

All those years later, I knew I would move to Florida. It was just a matter of when.

In January 2017, I flew to Tampa, Florida, where I first attended Dr. Joe Dispenza's Progressive and Advanced workshops. In his workshops, he taught us the science behind shifting our energy and led us through several meditations.

Between the two workshops, I had a two-day break, which I used to explore the Gulf side of Florida.

I was pleased to see that not every home was outrageously expensive like I'd thought they were in the Fort Lauderdale area. That gave me hope that I could afford to live somewhere in Florida, on my own, without having to have a bunch of extra jobs to make ends meet like I saw people doing when I visited Kauai. After exploring, I felt a strong knowing that I wanted to live on the Atlantic side of the state. I have always loved the sound of the rolling waves crashing in and lapping up against the sand. There's something powerful and healing about it for me. It calms and relaxes me and seems to magically make my worries insignificant, as if they're just a grain of sand instead of the mountain I made them out to be.

During the Advanced workshop, Dr. Joe took us through several meditation practices to reach a deeper level of understanding and experience. I wasn't a big meditator. I was a tapping geek and could tap for hours on end several times a week, but I was challenged doing this meditation for more than five minutes. The most meditating I'd done was in the few months prior, when I was preparing to attend the Progressive workshop.

I didn't know what to expect during the guided meditation he led us through. Almost every time I meditated, my mind raced and chattered away. I didn't think it counted as meditation to sit still, listening to my mind squawking. But I kept trying anyway after Dr. Joe repeated, "No meditation is a bad meditation."

The last two days of the retreat, Dr. Joe led us through a four-hour meditation at the butt-crack of dawn both mornings. I didn't know if I could do a four-hour meditation without having to get up to go to the bathroom. I heard others express the same concern, but then I heard some participants who had done it before say the time flew by and it wouldn't seem like four hours. I decided to give it a try. When my alarm went off at 3:00 a.m., I thought I was a little nuts, but I was determined to follow Dr. Joe's guidance and go for it.

While lying on the carpeted floor in the hotel ballroom with a padded eye mask covering my eyes and a thin cotton blanket spread over my body, I heard "Melbourne, Florida" quietly come into my mind. I felt a strong urge to move there. After the meditation, I felt calm and peaceful, and I was pleased I made it through four hours with ease. Then at breakfast, "Melbourne, Florida" came back into my mind. I dismissed it. I had never heard of Melbourne, Florida before. Although I didn't doubt its existence, I didn't know where it was on the map, I didn't know anybody there, and I'd never been there before. I just pooh-poohed it and stuck with the thought that I'd move to Fort Lauderdale.

After I returned home from the Advanced retreat, Melbourne was still on my mind. I googled it and found that it was on the Atlantic side of the state. It was southeast of Orlando by 75 miles and about 150 miles north of Fort Lauderdale. *Well, I will move somewhere between Fort Lauderdale and Melbourne,* I thought. But I was still leaning toward Fort Lauderdale, probably because it was familiar to me. In another meditation, I felt a strong clarity come over me that I was not to move to Fort Lauderdale. It felt like it was too rushed, too crowded, and too expensive.

Interestingly, a couple of my girlfriends had also received messages to move. Kim, my dear friend whom I had traveled to workshops with, was being guided to move to Maui. Laura, whom I had met through Kim, was being guided to move to San Diego, California. We jumped for joy with wide, shit-eating grins on our faces that each of us had received messages to move out of Minnesota to warm, tropical climates. *How lucky are we?* I happily thought.

The three of us formed a secret group with each other, because we weren't ready to share with others that we had received messages to move out of state. It seemed a little crazy to tell people that. We mainly communicated via text. But we also got together a couple of times in person to help each other with the next steps in our moves. We met at a coffee shop once and a restaurant another time. We helped one another process the realizations and emotions of things like the facts that we would be leaving our kids or had never been to the location we were moving to. We supported and encouraged one another through the tears, laughter, and excitement. We even tapped together to help let go of fears when they crept in.

I'd been telling my son, Craig, every winter for several years that I'd be moving to Florida. He probably didn't fully believe me because it only seemed like an annual cold-weather complaint. I didn't offer concrete details as far as timing or location or seem convinced myself that it was going to happen. I first brought it up more formally to him when we moved out of his childhood home and into our rental townhome. I told him I would be moving at some point after he finished high school, but I didn't know if I'd move closer to work or Florida, and he could move with me if he wanted. He said no to both options. He wasn't into hot weather, so Florida was never appealing to him; and he didn't want to move closer to my work. At that time, I wanted to believe I'd move to Florida, but I knew I had some fear inside about moving there by myself. It still seemed more like a vague dream. The next time I brought it up was a couple of years later, when he was nineteen years old and after I had received the message in the meditation. I told him that when our lease was up in October, I would be moving to Florida. It didn't seem to faze him until later, when he saw me taking actions and knew I was serious. It was no longer a cold-weather complaint or vague dream.

It wasn't the first time my boss, Doug Burrman, heard "moving to Florida" out of my mouth either. I had planted seeds about moving to warm and sunny Florida every winter with him too. But I dreaded telling my boss about my move. Not because I was afraid to talk to him, but because it was emotional for me. I knew, as a steward and the vice president of the family office, that I needed to say something to Doug so we could prepare the office for the change over the coming months. But I was nervous about telling him because I didn't have an exact date and I wasn't ready to resign. Not having all the facts hadn't stopped me before. This was quite different, though, because it impacted the management of the office, our relationship, and my employment. I, of course, tapped to clear out my emotions about having that conversation with him. That's when I realized it wasn't just fear about moving, but also sadness and concern about leaving him. The day I let him know that I would be moving to Florida in the fall, I was very calm and confident. I suggested we talk about grooming the administrative coordinator to manage the office.

TRUSTING MY GUIDANCE

A week later, while showcasing my EFT business at a psychic fair, I had an exciting experience. My booth space was in between two other booths, and the two business owners happened to be sisters. I had previously met Dotti, and I had just met Kristy for the first time that day. Kristy was offering quantum healings. She helped people shift the energy inside their bodies and provided them with messages from the Divine that helped them to receive clarity and be able to take the next steps in their lives. While she was working on other people, I could feel tingly electrical goosebumps run up my legs and into my body.

Oh my gosh, this is cool, I thought. *My body is tingling, and she isn't even working on me. I will be working with her later today, for sure!*

During our downtime, when we didn't have people at our booths, Kristy and I started to get to know each other. Without any hesitation, because of the healing work she does, I told her that Melbourne, Florida, came to me during a meditation as a place that I was supposed to move to, and I would be moving there toward the end of October when my lease was up.

When I sat down with her at the end of the day to experience my own quantum healing session, she eloquently phrased a message she received for me: "Be open to the opportunity to move as early as June."

If I'd had a drink of water in my mouth at that moment, I would have spit it out. I laughed. "Ha ha, yeah, right. *Opportunity.* Good one. That's a little too soon, to move in June."

The feeling in my body was calm, but the talk in my head was argumentative. My logical mental chatter was trying to run the show. *Pfft, that doesn't even make sense. My lease isn't up until October. Why would I move before then? Well, maybe I will go to Melbourne in June sometime to look for a place to live. That would be in the realm of possibility, but I couldn't move in June. That's way too soon.*

In the past, I wouldn't have noticed the calm feeling in my body and would have put more faith in what my logical mind was saying. I would have followed that because it made sense. I wouldn't have been open to trusting and following my guidance. It would have seemed too crazy and woo-woo.

But over the next couple of weeks, I continued to follow the urges I was feeling inside and took action as if I were moving midyear, while my mind was still in a bit of disbelief and thought June was too soon to move. Then I noticed I had started to talk as if I were going to move in June.

It was an interesting dichotomy between my logical mind and my guidance. Moving away from the comfort I'd known for my whole life felt both right and a little crazy at the same time. I had lived in Minnesota for all my life except for one year, when I lived in the neighboring state of Wisconsin. Everyone and everything familiar to me was in Minnesota. My nineteen-year-old son was there. My family, friends, co-workers, and clients were there. I grew up there and knew my way around. I knew the culture and the seasons of Minnesota weather. Now I was getting ready to pack my belongings and move by myself to a place where everything would be new and unknown to me.

The logical part of me thought it just didn't seem to make sense to move and leave all that behind. *Why would I move away from my boss and a great job that I enjoy that provides excellent pay and benefits? Why would I leave my clients that I love, especially after working so hard to build my business? Why in the world would I move away from my only child? And my family?*

That's when I realized I had to seriously stay out of my logical, thinking brain about the moving time frame, or else I would think I was crazy and would get in the way of making the move happen as guided.

I knew I couldn't think about any of that, and I had to trust the guidance I received. I couldn't sit and dwell on the fact that I wouldn't have any clients, family, or friends where I was moving. I didn't know what I was going to do for work. I stopped myself from thinking about all that. I had to let go over and over to surrender and trust the guidance that I had received to move.

I still felt apprehensive about sharing with some people that I was moving to Florida because it came to me in a meditation. I thought they would think I was nuts. I felt like I couldn't even articulate to my family exactly why I was moving now, even though they had heard me talk about moving to Florida for years. I could see how my decision to move in June might look crazy to them, mainly because life finally seemed to be going so well for me. They likely wondered what the hell I was doing, why I was leaving, or what I was running from. I wasn't running from anything; I was running to my new life that had been calling me for so long. I was running deeper into the connection with the Divine, running full speed ahead to connecting with my true self.

After I shared with my EFT clients that I'd received guidance and would be moving to Florida, my one-on-one client sessions on Fridays and Saturdays filled up back-to-back. The weekly tapping circles were fuller than ever, and on Tuesday evenings the group kept growing. My business was busier than ever before, and I understood exactly what was happening. My clients wanted to get in as many tapping sessions with me as possible before I moved, just like I had wanted to get in as many therapy sessions with Penny as possible before she had moved a couple of years earlier. I wanted to support them and tap as much as possible too.

So, in addition to working Monday through Thursday at my job, I tapped on Tuesday evenings, all day on Fridays, and on Saturday mornings. Sunday was my rest day, but somehow I had to fit packing into the mix.

THE BUSINESS PROPOSAL

Now I needed to go back to my boss to let him know I was moving sooner than October. Doug and I had been working together for almost eight years at this point and had successfully worked through a lot of different and difficult office situations together. I felt grateful to get to work with him. I knew he didn't want to lose someone who knew him so well and who he trusted to manage and take care of things the way he wanted them to be taken care of. Plus, I didn't want to stop working for him; nor was I prepared to stop working and go full-time with my coaching business.

So I spent a lot of time thinking through different options and getting clear on what my role as a remote employee could look like. I asked myself how I could best serve him and the office and came up with a plan to present to him. I used the same process I had used when I asked for that big raise.

On my drive to meet Doug for dinner at the North Oaks Golf Club, I felt an array of emotions. Nervousness was the easiest one to pinpoint, but I was honest with myself that I also felt scared because I didn't know if he would approve my idea of working remotely. I also felt sad because I knew that no matter how our conversation turned out, after I moved I wouldn't be connected to him Monday through Thursday in person as I had been for years. I would miss him. Before I got out of my car, I sat there for a moment, feeling my emotions and shifting myself into a space of feeling calm, confident, and grateful.

After we ordered our meals, it was time for me to open up and share the change with him. I felt emotion well up behind my eyes and a lump form in my throat as I told him I would be leaving sooner than I had first thought. I could see his eyes gloss up too, as he let me know that although he wanted me to stay, he understood I had other work to do in my life. Then he said, "Well, it gets sweltering in Florida in the summer. Maybe you shouldn't move in the summer."

I looked him in the eyes without saying a word.

"You're not moving because of weather, are you?" he said.

"No, Doug, I am not."

In all the years I had thought about moving to Florida, this was the first time I fully realized it wasn't about the weather. I mean, that was a great perk, but I was moving because I was guided to move, and he understood that on some level.

I was uncomfortable with all the emotions I felt coming up inside of me and quickly took a sip of water to get the tears to back off. Then I steered the conversation to talk about my business proposal of working remotely.

Doug's eyes lit up. "You'd be willing to do that?"

I nodded. "Yes, Doug, I am." I felt hopeful that he might accept my proposal. I told him I was interested in trying it and painted a picture of what I thought that could look like, just like I had practiced when I was preparing for our meeting.

First, I suggested that I step down from the responsibility of day-to-day manager and offer that part of my role to the person we were grooming for the role of office manager. Although I didn't want to take a pay cut, I suggested that too, so Doug could offer an increase of pay to the new office manager. We talked through everything on the business proposal document I provided to him and agreed we would give it a try as well as communicate along the way about how it was working. We decided we'd assess and revamp as needed. In my mind, I needed to serve him in the best possible way so he could see the value I provided to him, or he shouldn't be paying me.

I knew Doug needed more time to process all these changes, and we agreed not to let employees know yet. I felt like I was leading a double life for a while because I couldn't speak at work about my upcoming move. But when I felt like it was time to share my news publicly on social media, I let Doug know I needed him to share it with employees.

The morning after my son's twentieth birthday celebration, I flew to Florida to find my next home.

Chapter Thirteen

OUT OF MY HEAD
AND INTO MY HEART

FINDING MY WAY

I found a cute little Airbnb to stay in for the week while exploring Melbourne, Florida, in search of my new home. It was a comfortable, cozy one-bedroom home decked out in coastal decor. After I got settled, I looked over the list of rentals that my realtor, Wendy, had sent me ahead of time. I planned my first explorative adventure the next morning. I drove around to different areas to start familiarizing myself with Melbourne.

The following day, Wendy and I got together to scout for homes. We couldn't get the key out of the lockbox at the first place we stopped at, so we left. The next few places we looked at weren't fabulous at all. They had strange floor plans and weird, musty odors. As we started looking at rentals near the beach, I noticed the rental prices increased significantly while the square footage dropped. A couple of the beachside rentals we looked at still had decor from the 1960s and '70s, like big floral-print wallpaper or monkey-vomit green shag carpet. At one place, the master bathroom toilet seemed like an afterthought.

I was utterly frustrated that nothing we had looked at felt like home to me, and it didn't feel good to try to force a fit and pretend I liked something for the sake of feeling relief that I'd found a home.

On my way back to the Airbnb, I had an emotional meltdown that turned into a temper tantrum with God. I yelled and cried out, "You're the one who wants me to move here. I'm following your directions. I am packing up my whole life. Leaving my son. Leaving my family. Leaving my clients. I am looking for a home in Melbourne, just like you said. And I can't find a place to live. All the places I've looked at are shitholes. They feel uncomfortable. They aren't right for me. I don't know where I am. I don't know anyone here. If you want me to move here, then you need to show me where I'm supposed to be. Because this isn't working for me!"

I sobbed and continued pleading with God after not feeling immediate relief. "I'm doing what you want me to do. I'm following my guidance. I can't find a place, and I don't want to be shoved into a tiny shithole somewhere. I don't want to force myself into something that doesn't feel good. Help me out here, for fuck's sake!"

I felt overwhelmed in every sense of the word. I mean, there wasn't anything wrong with my life. If somebody looked at my life, they would think I had it made and wonder why the hell I was moving. At that moment, I was afraid of trusting my guidance, to leave all that, to move somewhere unknown without knowing why I was being guided to move. But because things weren't quickly and easily panning out like I thought they should, I knew I needed to follow, trust, and go with the flow.

The next day, I drove back across the bridge to the beachside, and around the corner I saw the yellow town house that was on my list. It was one of five town houses connected right across the street from the ocean. It even had an adorable short palm tree in the flower bed in front of the home.

That place is cute, I thought. *I'd like to look at the inside of it.* I circled it on my list so I could let Wendy know I was interested in checking it out.

Then I continued further south down State Road A1A to an area that felt nice and safe. There were four rentals to check out in the community. I took a closer look at the rental descriptions and saw two of them were seasonal rentals, so I crossed them off my list. The other two I drove by and then circled on my paper so Wendy and I could check them out along with the yellow town house. I was pleased I now had three rental town homes near the ocean that I felt good about and were in my budget. I wanted to set up times to see the insides of these homes. I drove out of that area and headed back north on A1A. As I was driving, I noticed I felt calm and relaxed inside my body.

Wow. It feels sooooo good right here. I took a deep breath in, turned my head to the left, and saw the yellow town home I had first circled on the list. *Oh, well, that's clearly a sign.*

Wendy and I both had already contacted the landlord a couple of days earlier but hadn't heard back yet. I had two criteria that might prevent me from living there: I needed two bedrooms, and they must allow two cats. If the rental didn't meet my requirements, then I wouldn't waste my time looking. I feared they weren't responding because they didn't allow cats.

On Wednesday morning, Wendy called me with good news. "We're in. They allow cats. We have a time to set up to go look."

ON THE OTHER SIDE

It was perfect, and I was thrilled. We met at the town house, and when we walked inside, we could see they had just painted it and installed brand-new carpet as well as new bathroom fixtures and ceiling fans. It looked like they had refurbished the inside. It felt fresh and clean. As I walked around, I imagined living there. I imagined the bedroom on the lower level as my office. I got geeky-excited when I looked out the upstairs living room windows and could see the ocean.

The home was a little smaller than my rental in Minnesota but perfectly sized for my kitties and me. Plus, it was right across the street from the ocean!

This is the place! I thought. I put in an application and was approved the very next day.

A CONNECTION OR TWO

While still in Melbourne, I wanted to find my community after finding my new home. I wanted to find a networking group, places that I could teach EFT, and a spiritual community where I could meet people to build friendships. I didn't want to move there a month and a half later without having another connection or two.

I looked on Meetup.com for different networking groups, spiritual groups, meditation groups, and various places I could connect with the types of people that I wanted to hang out with. There was a Meetup meditation group gathering at Unity of Melbourne that night for a love donation.

I arrived early at the church, and the lady leading it introduced herself as Jenny and said she was a hypnotherapist. I let her know I was following my guidance by moving to the area, and while in town I was trying to find my community and places where I could lead tapping workshops.

We talked for a bit. She was friendly, funny, and a wealth of knowledge; and our conversation was flowing as if we were long-lost friends. When it was time to start the meditation, we were the only two people there for it. I was enjoying my conversation with Jenny so much that I asked her if we could keep talking instead of doing the meditation. She agreed, and the two of us chatted away well past the scheduled meditation end time.

She shared her story of how she had moved to Florida from Ohio twelve years earlier. *Oh, she moved here by herself.* I thought. *I can do it too.* She also shared that she was on the Board of Directors at Unity of Melbourne, and the different rooms were available for rent. *Sweet!* I thought. *I have a connection and a place where I can tap.*

After serendipitously meeting Jenny, I was curious to see who else I would meet in the area. I looked on Meetup.com again and came across a healing and learning center called The Spark of Divine. Their calendar of events on Meetup.com listed weekly events, including yoga, reiki, and meditation. They also offered spiritual workshops led by different practitioners on a variety of topics like past life regression, understanding intuition, and Reiki 101. But I didn't see any EFT workshops listed. They had a psychic fair scheduled for Saturday, and I decided to check it out to see if it was a place where I would like to hold tapping workshops. If so, then I would connect with the owner and see if she would host workshops there.

On Friday night, I was catching up on classes and surveys I had missed during another Nancy Levin group coaching course I was taking, this time on relationships. I stayed up very late because I was in the groove, listening to the call replays and doing my homework. I didn't set the alarm for the next morning. I didn't need to wake up early, since the psychic fair started at 10:00 a.m. and my usual wake-up time was a lot earlier than that. When I woke, I sat in bed for a while, reading a book. I looked over at the time and was surprised.

Oh my gosh, it's ten already! Julie, you've got to get your lazy ass up, I scolded myself. *Hurry up and get ready. Get yourself to that event ASAP!* I fell into an old thought pattern then. I thought I was lazy because I was still in my pajamas around ten o'clock, and their event was starting. According to my inner dialogue, I was late, and I needed to get up, get ready, and have breakfast right now. But I recognized I was being hard on myself, and I changed my inner dialogue.

No, Julie, you're not lazy. You were up late, working on homework. You decided to not set the alarm, and when you got up you read for a while. Those are all good things, and you're taking care of yourself. You're not being lazy. You have plenty of time. You can still take your time getting ready, enjoy breakfast, and then make your way to the psychic fair. You don't need to be at the event a full day. You just need to go there for maybe an hour or so. Chill out and set the intention you'll arrive at the perfect time to connect with the perfect people.

After taking my time and enjoying my breakfast, I drove south down US Highway 1 from Melbourne through a cute little town called Sebastian down to Vero Beach with a massive smile on my face. My driver's side window was rolled down, and I could feel the wind in my hair with my radio blaring as I was singing and dancing in my seat. I was excited at the thought that I would soon be living here.

Just as I had intended, I arrived at the perfect time because I didn't have to wait long for an angel reading before Beth took me into the room, guided me over to the table on the far left, and introduced me to Marchelle. I sat down in the open chair in front of her table. We greeted each other, and then she closed her eyes and started to tune in to my energy. I sat quietly, noticing that Marchelle's brown hair touched her shoulders and was pulled back out of her face, showcasing her beautiful smile and cute dimples. She had a calm presence and radiant glow. When she opened her eyes, her lips were moving to form words, but sound wasn't coming out at first. She fanned her face with her hand, let out a sigh, and said, "You have a beautiful white light all around you and are surrounded by angels. It's overwhelming to see all of them, but in a good way."

She started to ask me a question. "Have you gotten . . ." But before she could finish the sentence, she began to ask a second question. "Have you started training?" Then she interrupted that question with a third. "You're supposed to be a healer if you're not already. Are you a healer?"

I calmly nodded and smiled as I told Marchelle I was an EFT practitioner. I knew what she was experiencing was good, and it felt like another confirmation for me. Her face lit up with a big smile. Her eyes moved from side to side as she tried to find words to describe what she was experiencing. But she was still having a hard time completing a sentence before the next one started coming out. "You are . . . big changes . . . You have some significant changes coming your way," she said.

I confirmed, "Yes, I am following my guidance. I received

in a meditation in February that I am to move to Melbourne, Florida. So now I am in town, finding a place to live as well as my community of people and places where I could teach EFT workshops. I will be moving from Minnesota at the end of June."

"Ah. That's why these angels are all around you." Marchelle smiled even wider, and with a gleam in her eye she said, "And coincidently, I am the owner of a place in Sebastian where you can hold workshops. It's about fifteen minutes north of The Spark of Divine, called Into the Mystic. You probably passed it on your way here. It's right across the street from Wendy's restaurant. Look for it on your way back." She gave me her business card and told me to call her after I got settled so we could get together for lunch and schedule some EFT workshops. I thanked her. We hugged goodbye like we were long-lost friends, and I told her I would be in touch. I tucked her card in my purse.

On my way out of the psychic fair, I stopped to talk with the owner of The Spark of Divine. "Beth, thank you for putting together this event. It was fun. I enjoyed connecting with Marchelle. She was the perfect person for me to get a reading from! You have a nice shop here too."

"Thank you, Julie," said Beth. "We'd love to have you back."

"I will be back. I am moving from Minnesota to Melbourne Beach at the end of June. I am an EFT practitioner. Are you open to holding EFT workshops here?"

Beth happily replied with a smile that she was familiar with EFT. She had a friend who did it as well. Her friend didn't hold any workshops, but even if she did, Beth believed there was enough for everyone. She said she'd love to have me hold EFT workshops there. I thanked her again and let her know

I would be in touch with her after I got settled. I tucked her business card in my purse next to Marchelle's.

On my way back to the Airbnb, I laughed to myself. *Well, that couldn't have unfolded any better if I had planned it.*

I had listened to my inner guidance, and as a result I had connected with woo-woo spiritual people just like me. It all showed that it was not up to me to decide where, when, and how I lived my life, but it was my job to trust and follow my guidance.

FOR MY CLOSURE

Several years before I moved to Florida, there were lessons I had learned that helped me with that time. A couple of years after the 2008 recession, I filed for bankruptcy. My home was included in it and completely discharged, which meant I no longer owned the house but could remain living there as long as I paid the monthly mortgage payment. I did that for four years. It was during those four years that our neighborhood shifted so much that I no longer felt safe or comfortable living there.

I used to know almost all my neighbors by name. We would greet each other over at the mailboxes, and they would wave as I drove around the bend to my garage. Many of them moved after short selling or foreclosing on their homes. So I didn't know my new neighbors' names and rarely saw them outside. There were often drug dealers instead of kids sitting in the town house complex park that I could see out my kitchen window. There was also an increased police presence in what used to be a quaint little area.

It was at that time that I made a difficult decision and chose to go through the foreclosure process. I was in a strange predicament. My house was upside down by at least $50,000 as a result of the housing crash during the recession. Because my name was still on the mortgage, the only way I could get my name off if I wanted to move was to short sell or foreclose on the house. But because the home was part of the bankruptcy, the bank wasn't allowed to talk to me, so that eliminated the short sell option.

Most people assume foreclosure is negative, but I chose to make it a favorable decision and dubbed that time in my life "For My Closure." Not only was I foreclosing on my home and preparing to move, but I was also closing my jewelry business and decluttering my home. Although it was emotional, it was also a good and happy time for me.

I wasn't sure exactly how long we would have, but I knew my son, Craig, and I had several months to prepare to move out of the home that he had grown up in. By renting, I could move into a community I felt safer in and position myself to move closer to work after my son finished with school. Or even to Florida, if I dared to move there by myself.

When we were preparing to move, I looked around my house and got a little choked up as I realized there wasn't a lot in it that I loved—or even really liked, for that matter. When I first moved into that home and money was tight as a newly single mom, I had purchased a light beige couch and matching love seat because they were on sale in a price range I could afford. I thought they were "good enough," and I would get something better down the road when I could afford it. Now, here it was, thirteen years later, and I had the same couch and love seat that I never really liked.

I looked at the decor I had hanging on my living room walls and found the same theme over and over. But it wasn't a theme of style. It was a theme of shoulds. *I should hang that because so-and-so gave it to me. I should buy that because it's on sale or because it's good enough for now.* My ex-husband and his wife had given me a cross for Christmas one year, and I thought I should hang it up even though I didn't like it. I had hung it so my son would know that I was acknowledging his father. Plus, it was a cross. What would I do with a cross if I didn't hang it up? I didn't know. It wasn't like I could throw a cross in the garbage or a box somewhere; it felt too sacred. So I had hung it up on my wall, and I subconsciously cringed every time I saw it.

My birth mother had also given me some decor that matched the beige couch and love seat I didn't ever really like. Although the wall hangings of the Eiffel Tower and the Big Ben clock were cool, they were in drab colors that didn't feel good to me. I had hung those up on my wall too.

I looked at the decor in my living room, which mainly consisted of items other people had given to me. Although they had given the decorations to me with love and good intention and I had appreciated their generosity, I didn't love or even like many of the items. At the time I received the gifts, I had felt like I needed to display them or put them on the wall simply because someone had given them to me. I hadn't taken into consideration whether I liked the items or not, and it hit me kind of hard that I didn't even know who I was or what I liked after all those years.

I did have a couple of framed horse paintings I loved, but they reminded me of my ex-husband. We had purchased them together at the Minnesota Renaissance Festival in celebration of our anniversary. Having stuff in my home that was part of a marriage that had ended in divorce wasn't good energy, according to my dear friend, Kim, who was a feng shui consultant. That made sense to me because I thought of our anniversary and subsequent divorce whenever I looked at those, which kept me attached to my past. It was time to get rid of them as I moved into this new phase of my life.

Down in my basement, I had a studio where I created and kept gorgeous, handmade, beaded jewelry. Up against the wall, I had two wide, tall, brown bookcases with adjustable shelves that were filled top to bottom with containers of beads. To the right of the bookshelves, in the storage area underneath the staircase, were neatly stacked, sturdy, blue plastic totes filled with items to display jewelry. Although I loved many of the beads and had, for the most part, enjoyed my jewelry business over ten years, I was closing it down and wanted to sell all my inventory and display items before I moved. I didn't want to take them with me into my new place. It was time to let all this go, for my closure.

Although I was moving to a place with more square footage, I still realized that I didn't need or want all these things anymore. Something was shifting inside me; I no longer wanted all these material items or tolerated items that didn't feel good to me.

The process of letting go before the move proved to be a big release in a few different ways. After I moved into my new home, I began to see how the energy of items had affected me. When I walked into my old house and didn't like that cross hanging up on the wall or didn't enjoy those pictures hanging above the couch that I didn't like, a little part of me twinged inside. Every. Single. Time. It didn't feel good in my home, and I didn't even like to have people over because of it. I was tolerating things in my house out of obligation or because it had been "good enough" at an affordable price. I hadn't realized it, but I had been busy numbing those yucky, twinging feelings out; and eventually, I had completely blocked them out, which mirrored what I had done with the abuse: twinged, numbed, and blocked it out. But what I had found was that it took energy to block out all those tolerations—and what a waste of energy that had been.

THE LOVE RULE

I was often sick when I lived in that home. I was tired. I had a hard time getting up in the mornings. Those items decorating my home impacted how I felt on so many levels. When I started making decisions for my new home with my personal preferences in mind, I started feeling relieved and energized, which in hindsight made so much sense to me because everything is energy and impacts us in some way.

I wanted to leave it with my old life when I moved out of my home. So I made a rule for myself: nothing could go into the new home unless I loved it. Period. And I meant LOVE, not just like. That was the rule I used to guide myself to make decisions about every single item I owned. Would I move it with me, or let it go?

If I didn't love it, then I sold it at garage sales or through Facebook and Craigslist. And then, when I ran out of time to sell things and didn't want those items entering our new home, I donated them to Goodwill. I took the money from the items I sold and put it aside to purchase furniture and decor for the new house. I didn't have a couch and a love seat anymore; it was time for a new bed frame and mattress, and I wanted some beautiful wall decorations that inspired me.

Although I was an excellent jewelry maker and easily mixed a variety of colors and styles of beads to create stunning pieces that women oohed and aahed over, that creative eye didn't transfer over to interior decorating. So I enlisted my girlfriend, Pam, to help me decorate the new home. She's one of those people who can visualize where things would go in the house and how exactly they would be used, whereas I couldn't necessarily see where to put something or how to make it practical unless it was something I was specifically looking for and knew where I wanted to put it.

Pam helped me shop for items that I loved. We went to different stores together, and she would point out items and ask me if I liked them. Sometimes before I even spoke, she would see my facial expression and put the pieces back before I could articulate myself. For example, when she picked up a basket with green and yellow accents, my nose scrunched up. The shape of the basket was cute, but the colors were not for me in my home.

Other times, there were items she'd show me, and my face would light up. She found a teal and brown lamp that was the perfect height for my teal entry accent cabinet. Before I could answer, she said she was putting it in the cart because yes was written all over my face.

I applied what I learned from Pam and my Love Rule when shopping on my own. I found a beautiful metal butterfly with a two-foot wingspan that matched the colors of my new quilt. Butterflies are meaningful to me because they symbolize transformation. I got one tattooed on my right shoulder after my divorce and several years later included a butterfly as part of my business logo. The metal butterfly was pretty and meaningful, and it fit perfectly above my headboard. I also found a gorgeous antique stationery desk, repainted in turquoise. My eyes lit up when I first spotted it. It spoke to me, and I had to have it. I ended up using it to store my greeting cards, envelopes, and stationery. Since I was a little kid, when my grandma was my penpal, I always had stationery and notecards on hand. I still regularly handwrite messages to friends and mail them. So the piece of furniture is a color I love, fits who I am, is useful, and makes me smile.

After the decorations were up, visitors' reactions were always the same. They took a deep breath in and said, "Wow, it feels so good in here." I realized it was because, for the first time, the items represented me and therefore felt good to others. The energy in my new space was very supportive of me, and I was excited to invite guests into my home.

That was a massive shift for me.

When I went shopping, I questioned every item. *Do I love this? And where in my home is it going? How will I use it?* Little did I know I was also preparing for my next move. When I purchased decor for my temporary rental in Minnesota, it was actually for my Florida home because the colors and style were a coastal theme. All I was doing was purchasing items that brought me joy and felt good.

When I packed up to move to Florida, I applied the rule again and also paid attention to if I needed each item in Florida, and if I had space for it in my smaller home.

The rule still applies in my life today. Items don't come home unless I love them. When I'm out shopping, before I check out at the register I check in with myself to make sure

I love the items before I buy them. Previously it was too easy for me to buy stuff on clearance because I liked it well enough and couldn't pass up the deal. That type of decision-making doesn't cut it for me anymore. If I like it but don't love it, even though it's a good deal, it's not coming home. Period. The rule is, I MUST love it!

Every object has energy, including everything in our homes. So as things that make me feel good surround me, that brings up my energetic vibration. My home is cozy, comfortable, and feels lovely because the energetic tone of anything that comes into my home is love. When I look around my own home, I love the way I have it decorated in a coastal theme. I love how I feel there.

Chapter Fourteen

THE STORM

A STORM APPROACHES

In September of 2017, just a couple of months after I had moved to Florida, Hurricane Irma wreaked havoc in the Caribbean and then headed straight for Florida. I hadn't ever been through a hurricane before. In Minnesota, I'd been through a few blizzards that closed the city down for a day or two as well as scarily destructive tornadoes, but never a hurricane. When I heard the Category 5 hurricane was pointed my way, I decided to evacuate because I lived right across the street from the ocean and didn't see any reason to stay for the storm's unwelcomed intrusion.

My neighbors informed me that if I left the barrier island where I live, the causeways back over to the island would be blocked off once the hurricane passed through. No traffick would be allowed through, even for residents, to help prevent looting and unnecessary injuries. The town officials would reopen them once the debris was picked up and it was safe for residents to drive on the streets again. The only way I would be able to get across the bridge then was if I had proof that I lived there.

Uh-oh! I thought. *I haven't applied for my Florida driver's license yet.* I wondered what the heck to do. Feeling tension creep into my shoulders, I took a deep breath in to calm down and think it through. Then I added my lease, utility bill, and water bill to my packing checklist if I needed proof that I lived there to get back home.

It took a few days to prepare for my departure, which proved to be the most challenging and exhausting part of the entire hurricane experience. Even with the high probability that the hurricane could weaken before making landfall, it was a crapshoot. I had to prepare for the worst while hoping for the best. I lived alone and had to make these life decisions about everything by myself. In a frantic, panicked state, I ran up and down the stairs several times, trying to figure out what to pack and where to put my stuff because a Category 5 hurricane could demolish my home and everything in it.

I just moved here, I thought. *God guided me to this location. Now I don't know if I will have a home to return to after the hurricane.* I took time to tap on the stress I felt swirling through my body. I needed to breathe and calm myself down again and again so I could purposefully pack things in preparation for the different possible scenarios.

I reasoned that if the overall structure of the home survived but the ocean water made its way across the street, then my office could flood. *What do I need?* I asked myself. *Hard-to-replace items. Okay, what are those?* I carefully packed tax documents and printed photos in big blue plastic storage bins and hauled them upstairs. I then inserted the bins into large, white heavy-duty plastic garbage bags for extra protection; then duct-taped them shut and put them into the second closet in my bedroom. It was emotionally and physically tiring.

After I had those items secured in the upstairs closet, I took time to breathe and calmly think through my next steps.

Since I had no way of knowing how long I would be gone or

what condition I would find my home in when I returned, and I only had so much space in my small SUV for my items, I had to decide what was most important to take with me. I could feel my heart beating faster as I thought about the roof blowing off my townhouse and my papers and photos flying in the hurricane wind. I sat down on my bed and tapped again while focusing on those thoughts and feelings to calm back down. A few minutes later, I was able to think through all the items in my home. I started piling things to take in the downstairs hallway, like the two kitty carriers and their essentials. I gathered important documents that were not easily replaceable, like my passport and vehicle registration. I also loaded a thumb drive with tax documents and account passwords.

Then I thought about the items most often sent to hurricane victims, including toiletries, and I packed them. I selected foods from my cupboards like nuts and bars that needed no refrigeration to keep or stove to prep in case we didn't have power. I packed up all my bottles of water, plus candles, flashlights, and batteries. And I packed my computer, monitors, laptop, and all the necessary cords, because I didn't want to have to replace those items either.

After packing, I looked around and thought, *Everything else just doesn't matter or can easily be replaced if I need it.*

I hugged my neighbors goodbye; put my cats, Dexter and Gizmo, in their carriers in the car; filled up my gas tank; and headed north to Orlando, Florida, to stay with a friend, Bev, and her family. Even though her son was extremely allergic to cats, they welcomed my kitties and me into their home. We had a bedroom to ourselves, away from her son's room, that the kitties stayed in 24/7. I set out a couple of their favorite small toys and a blanket to help them feel the comforts of home when I wasn't in the room with them.

We stayed at Bev's for about five days—before, during, and after the hurricane. It helped keep my nerves calm to be with her family because they had lived through hurricanes and knew what to expect. I took their advice over well-intentioned, non-hurricane-experienced family and friends' unsolicited and sometimes panicked advice.

We all knew and agreed not to get caught up in watching the news frenzy. We only turned the TV on for brief updates every four or five hours to see where the hurricane was heading, what intensity level it was at, and when it was expected to make landfall because those factors were continually changing.

We worked together, battening down the hatches and bringing in potted plants and outdoor furniture. The hurricane was still at least a day away, but stores and restaurants were closing down in the area. We stayed home, played board and card games, shared stories, and laughed a lot. Not to mention we amusingly talked ourselves into eating lots of ice cream because it could melt should the power go out.

I stayed connected on Facebook so family and friends would know where I was and how I was doing. In my Facebook feed, I was happy to see a group meditation scheduled online with the intention to send love and healing energy to the hurricane. I joined online because, after my meditation experiences at Dr. Joe Dispenza's retreat, I believed our intentions and energy could help reduce the hurricane's intensity and shift its path. I followed along on the twenty-minute worldwide guided meditation, breathing in and out of my heart while focusing on love. Even if it didn't work, it sure felt good to calm my mind and body and send love out into the world. Afterward, I turned the news on to find the intensity of the hurricane had shifted and lowered from a Category 4 to a Category 3. The meditation had been so exciting to participate in, so I continued to send love to Hurricane Irma throughout the storm.

IRMA'S AFTERMATH

The night that Hurricane Irma made landfall in Orlando, it jarred me awake. The howling winds sounded like a loud freight train right outside the window, and the pounding rain sounded like someone was throwing buckets of water on the roof nonstop. With only an occasional meow, Dexter and Gizmo quietly huddled together under the bed.

For a few minutes, I felt scared, not knowing how much worse it would get; and I wanted to huddle under the bed with the cats too. But when I shifted my thoughts to enjoy the sounds of the hurricane instead, it wasn't as bad as I imagined it would be. The house wasn't even shaking or anything like that. After a short while, I closed my eyes and focused my attention on sending love to the ferocious hurricane. That simple act calmed my insides down, and I fell back to sleep before it was over.

The next morning, I woke and found out Irma had passed through with little damage to the area. I was so grateful she had calmed slightly by the time she reached Bev's. Although the electricity was out, branches were down, the neighbors' fences knocked over, and some roofs were taken off, I was grateful we were all safe and sound. Afterward, the baffling part for me was grappling with how things almost seemed anticlimactic after the week-long, stressful frenzy of prepping and waiting for the hurricane to hit while knowing other parts of Florida had taken the brunt of her wrath and gotten utterly pummeled.

By the fifth day of my stay at Bev's, she and her husband and son were starting to get a little testy with each other. The hurricane had already passed, the power had been off for a couple days, and it was hot and humid. We didn't know when the electricity would be back on. I thought that would be a perfect time for me to exit because I didn't want anything negative to happen to my relationship with any of them. I found a hotel in the area that had power and allowed animals, so I booked a room for a few nights. I didn't know how long I would be there because it was dependent on when the electricity got turned back on at home. I set up my desktop computer and monitors on the desk in my room and focused on a work project so I wouldn't have to use up my remaining paid vacation time.

A few days later, I received word from my dear realtor friend, Wendy, that the electricity back home was on, and the causeways had reopened. After a total of ten days away, I headed back home. I could feel my face frowning and my eyelids drooping because it was sad to see the damage as I drove south on I-95. I noticed that the leaves on the trees were brown from the water and wind relentlessly beating on them for hours. The fields were flooded, roofs were missing from the tops of homes, business signs were damaged or missing, and debris was everywhere. I felt like I was in an old western movie where the tumbleweed was blowing down the deserted main street of a small town and a gunfight was about to go down.

When I arrived home, I left Dexter and Gizmo in the running, air-conditioned car as I checked everything out to make sure it was safe for them. I cautiously walked through every area of my home, looking for any damage; and I only found a little water upstairs on the kitchen and bathroom floors. The skylights were damaged during the hurricane but only leaked a little from the rain after the storm. That was it. I fell to my knees, crying when I found everything intact, and thanked God for no damage to my home. I felt all the stress from the past ten days leave my body.

MY BACK IS TO THE OCEAN

After that hurricane, something else shifted inside me that had me evaluating my life yet again. During the last couple of months before the hurricane hit, I had been working remotely in my home office with my back to the window, and it didn't feel good. I was right across the street from the ocean, but I felt trapped in my chair at my desk as I was doing my job.

I had failed to research in advance the pitfalls and tips for success for working remotely. The communication with the team wasn't going well.

I was still the vice president and expected to have a pulse on everything at the office in Minnesota, but it didn't feel like I did anymore. The office manager started making decisions without talking to me, and they weren't her decisions to make. I wasn't kept fully in the loop with work projects or interactions that were going on in the office. I was living the expression "out of sight, out of mind." I felt so much inner turmoil about having to sit at my desk to do my job, and it just didn't make sense anymore. But I didn't know what to do.

I felt disconnected from my boss and team. But more importantly, I felt disconnected from myself. When I got very honest with myself, it was clear it was no longer working for me to work this way.

I reached out to Nancy Levin again for one-on-one coaching to help me create a plan to leave my job. She had experienced a similar situation in her career. She had set herself up for success before leaving her event director role at Hay House, a mind-body-spirit publishing company. So I knew she could help me do the same. I told her I wanted to stay in my role a while longer as I built up my coaching business. I also wanted to make sure the office manager had adequate training. Nancy and I started working together over the phone.

"Julie, tell me what you'd like to work on today," Nancy said.

I automatically started tapping on the top of my head and through the same tapping points like I do during every coaching call. I confessed, "I am not putting in my exact hours each week at work since I moved to Florida. I feel guilty, like I am doing something wrong even though I crank through work a lot faster from home because I don't have the interruptions."

I paused before continuing. "And I just don't know how much longer I can do this. My back is to the ocean, and I feel chained to my desk. I didn't move down here to feel like this."

Nancy asked, "What's keeping you there?"

I replied, "I like working with my boss. I like working on the projects, and I don't want to lose my pay and benefits. It has a certain sense of security to it." Feeling a little panicky, I continued, "And I haven't started tapping workshops or circles since I moved here a couple of months ago. I feel like I'm having to start over with finding tapping clients after leaving Minnesota."

Nancy guided me to close my eyes, breathe into my heart, and go within, where the answers are always found. I stopped tapping for a moment while I did that. I could feel my heart slow its beating down and my shoulders relax as I moved my attention out of the fear in my head and into my heart. She reminded me to let the answers come and to jot them down or speak them out loud after I floated back up.

I opened my eyes and shared, "The truth is, no job is safe and secure. Any job could go away at any time. I am doing a good job with my work quality and quantity as well as meeting my deadlines. It's just the structure that is different, and I am still adjusting to it."

Then I told Nancy that I realized I had a fear that if I quit my job and went out on my own, I would flop like last time. I knew that was an irrational fear because, compared to the previous time, I now had zero debt, I had a large emergency fund, and I was a great coach and EFT practitioner. The fears weren't even real, but I still felt them as if they were. I assigned myself homework, confirming with Nancy, "I know I have to work through the emotions to get on the other side of the fear, so I will tap and clear it out."

"Great!" she exclaimed. "Text me when you're done, and let me know how you feel."

We hung up the phone. I felt relief and knew I had more work to do, so I stayed seated and started tapping through it right then.

A few weeks later, even though I felt better about the work I was doing, I still felt restless about having my back to the ocean. So in November, just before the week of Thanksgiving, I requested the full week off to spend time thinking about my life. I asked myself where I wanted to be down the road and if vice president was still the right role for me. Before this move, I thought I'd work for my boss for several years to come, but I was no longer sure that was true for me. I thought about my boss and how much I cared for him. I wanted him to be taken care of and felt very concerned that wouldn't happen at the level of service he had come to expect and rely on. That bothered me greatly. So to think about leaving didn't feel good, but thinking about staying felt worse.

It was a significant internal conflict. I was emotional about so many things that had happened at the family office over the years. During that week off, I took a lot of time to process many emotions. My dear friend, Patti, who had helped me tap on worthiness, agreed to tap with me over the phone. We tapped a few hours together, and I tapped for several more hours on my own on the emotions about whatever came up in my mind around the past family office situations.

Just like letting go of physical items before I moved to a new home, I needed to let go of mental and emotional interactions from the previous eight years at work so I could move on. I needed to tap on the frustrations from the impact Kit's behaviors had had on me as well as the disbelief and disappointment from dealing with Les. I tapped and tapped and tapped to clear out past issues with a list of people I had worked with at the family office over the years. I didn't realize that as I was tapping, I was letting go in preparation to let go even more. But that was precisely what happened next.

After tapping, my heartbeat slowed, and my breathing evened out. Clarity came, as it always does. I knew I needed to stop working in the capacity I was working in now, not later. It was hard to serve my boss and team well while working remotely in my role, and the reality was it wasn't working well. The office manager and I weren't communicating well with each other. I thought it was important that we work through our challenges even though it was uncomfortable, but it felt like she wanted to ignore them, just like I used to do. But I couldn't do that any longer.

So, I asked myself questions like, *What do I want?* I answered myself too. *I still want to work for my boss. I feel I can still add value to him by working on particular projects.* Because of my history, knowledge, and experience, I knew it was in the realm of possibility he would be open to employing me as a consultant to work on different projects for him. Now I needed to figure out which projects, how often I would work, and how much to charge as a consultant.

I had never been a consultant in this capacity before. During my next one-on-one coaching session with Nancy, she helped me first get connected to my heart and then walked me through some of the logical steps with information I needed to consider. And as usual, I tapped, starting on the top of my head, as we worked through the logical steps. Nancy didn't require me to tap; I knew from all my tapping experience and continuously tapping through the points on previous calls that it helped me process my fears faster.

Nancy guided me: "Julie, first, you'll need to figure out how much you need to cover all your expenses and then some."

I liked that she said "and then some" because in the past I would have said "enough to cover" and left it at that, not thinking about breathing room or that I was worthy to receive more. This time around, I wasn't willing to feel the stress of living paycheck to paycheck with "just enough." Been there, done that, not doing it again. Unsurprisingly, I felt resistance inside my body and shared it with Nancy. She helped me reveal the limiting belief that "I am not going to have enough" was trying to get in the way of making this necessary change happen.

THE TRUTH WAS

Years earlier, after I got laid off from my previous job and worked so many hours on my jewelry and travel businesses, I ended up broke and in bankruptcy. Although my life was very different now, the old beliefs and fears about not being able to make it on my own were creeping in. I shared those crappy thoughts with Nancy and told her that one had to go. I self-assigned my homework again: to tap on that crap.

When we got off the phone, I was excited instead of fearful. I knew I just needed to do my work and would be ready for that conversation with Doug in no time. I walked myself through the process I'd used when I asked for a substantial raise. I first addressed my fears of moving to a consultant role and having that be my primary source of income until I built up my business. Then I addressed my limiting belief about being worthy of charging at a consultant rate.

Like always, I started tapping on the top of my head and had a conversation with myself to start. As I made my way through the tapping points on my face, collarbone, and underarm, I noticed an uncomfortable sensation in my chest. I closed my eyes to tune into that space in my body, focused my attention on how it felt, and kept tapping. And as usual, after just a few minutes of tapping a couple of rounds, I felt relief.

After addressing the emotional concerns, I switched over to the logical side and ran the numbers. I landed in the perfect place for myself, an amount I felt comfortable asking for that was reasonable and would more than meet my needs. Next, I knew that I couldn't have expectations of Doug accepting my proposal and that I had to be completely unattached to the outcome, just like I had been before I had asked for that big raise. It's part of any good negotiation to be able to walk away. I had to get to that place even though I didn't want to walk away. I tapped several rounds through the points until I knew this or something better would work out for me.

All right, God, I prayed. *I hear you. I know I'm supposed to resign, and the thought of not being in that role gives me relief. I expect a miracle now. If I'm ending that role, then, God, I am trusting there's some miracle that's going to happen to bring income into my life. It may or may no longer be through the family office. It may be something completely different. And so I'm gonna let go of what it will look like. I'm going to present an option, but I'm going to let go of any attachment to that.*

Letting go and trusting was still challenging. I had previously wanted to control everything, but because I had experienced the freedom on the other side after letting go, it was getting more natural for me to do that.

I set up a time to talk with Doug on the Monday after Thanksgiving. Just as I had done before, I chose to feel calm, confident, and grateful during our call. Even with all the work I had done, it was a very emotional call for me as I shared my challenges and what I needed to do. I was open with him and let him know it was challenging for me to work remotely. I told him I didn't feel like I was serving him well, the communication wasn't good with the team, and I needed more freedom with my time. I said I needed to be done working as an employee by the end of the year. I cried way more than I thought I would as I resigned, but it was because I cared about Doug. I want him to be well-cared-for by his employees and hoped that would happen.

Doug was taken aback. He was quiet for a moment before he told me he didn't want me to leave and didn't like hearing that I needed to stop working there. After a few moments of silence, just like I had done when I had asked for the raise, I switched the conversation to present the idea of a contract to him. I said, "You, of course, can say no to this. It has to be a win-win for both of us, and we can talk through details if you're open to this."

I shut up to let him take it in, just like Bo Eason had said to do when onstage.

After being quiet for some time, he told me what I had shared with him sounded doable, but he needed a couple of days to process and think about it.

"Yes, of course," I said, and I asked him when he'd like me to follow up with him. He said a couple of days. *A couple of days*, I thought. *I can absolutely wait a couple of days.*

We hung up the phone, and I felt a surge of energy inside me and couldn't help but jump up to dance and cheer. My cats looked at me funny as I happy-danced around the living room, belting out, "Woooooo-hoooooo! Freedom!!!" I texted Nancy and let her know I had just given my notice and asked for a consultant contract. She responded with congratulations and a lot of expressive emojis.

Reflecting on all that had transpired, I concluded that it's essential to take time for ourselves. When we're feeling off inside, that's when taking time away to ask ourselves questions and get clarity is oh so important. I'm happy I did that. I felt better afterward and was able to trust I could expect a miracle. I took a step in faith by following that good feeling.

It was important to tell myself the truth about how I was feeling. And the truth was, I no longer was serving my boss well. I no longer wanted to be a manager and deal with the emotional crap that employees weren't willing to take responsibility for. The truth was, I wasn't a fit for the role anymore—and I needed to leave as an employee.

The old Julie would have just sucked it up and thought that I should stay working for my boss. She would have just plowed through it. She would have beat herself up and said things like, "You should be grateful you have this job. You love working for Doug. You make great money and have great benefits. You should stay. He needs you there."

But the new Julie knew she had to follow her guidance to let go of the good to allow in the great.

Chapter Fifteen
ANONYMOUS

THE LETTER

I was still feeling on top of the world after giving my notice at work, and I happy-danced my way down to the front door and outside to the mailbox. I had a pile of mail, but one letter caught my attention and curiosity. It didn't have a return address label and was from Saint Paul, Minnesota.

I thought the white envelope looked a little strange, so I examined it carefully. Off to the right side of the label, my address was handwritten in thick black marker on the envelope. I assumed someone from the post office had written my address in the marker because the faded, tiny, black, typed font on the white label was very difficult to read. My last name was spelled incorrectly: J-a-c-k-i-e instead of J-a-c-k-y. The return address space on the upper left corner of the envelope was blank, and the black metered post office stamp in the top right corner indicated it had been mailed from Saint Paul, Minnesota, on November 22, 2017.

It didn't strike me as strange to receive a letter from Saint Paul, Minnesota. But something felt odd about this.

I haven't given my new address out to very many people yet, I thought. *And a friend would spell my last name correctly. I wonder who sent this.*

I opened the envelope, pulled out a piece of white paper, unfolded it, and saw a typewritten letter. My eyes moved to the bottom of the page in search of a name, but nothing was there. No name. No signature. Nothing.

As I read the first sentence in all capital letters at the top of the page, my mouth dropped open.

What the fuck? I wondered. *Who the fuck wrote this? What are they talking about? This is really strange and creepy.*

My mouth was still dropped open and my eyes opened wide in disbelief. As I continued reading, I experienced a myriad of emotions as the anonymous writer accused me of some crazy things, including being partially responsible for the death of Les, Doug's long-time friend and former consultant.

"Are you fucking kidding me? I am not responsible for his death," I shouted.

I was dumbfounded and amazed, as I'd never received anything so mean and horrible like this before. I kept reading. It didn't get any better. I felt fear pulse through my body, as if I were being terrorized and threatened in my new home.

I was so upset that I called Doug, I didn't know if he'd answer or not because we didn't have a scheduled call. But we had just gotten off the phone thirty minutes earlier, so I hoped he'd still be available.

He greeted me, "Hello, Julie."

Out of breath and holding back tears the best I could, I said, "Doug, I just received an anonymous letter in the mail that is so hateful." I paused to push the tears back more. "I am being accused of contributing to Les's death."

I proceeded to read the whole letter to him in its entirety, exactly as written.

ANONYMOUS

I WANT YOU TO KNOW THAT I HAVE HAD
SEVERAL CONVERSATIONS ABOUT YOU OVER
THE YEARS EVEN THOUGH WE HAVE NEVER
MET. BELOW IS A LIST OF THINGS I HAVE
HEARD FROM LES WILSON WHICH HAS ALSO
BEEN CONFIRMED BY MANY OTHERS.

You sandbag your employees

You manage in FEAR

At one point all your employees were looking for new
jobs to get away from you, and Les said he even told
you this.

You are a FRAUD, and anyone who has it together is
a threat to you because they can quickly see that

You poured water on the floor, and blamed it on
Samantha's new puppy because that puppy could tell
you had EVIL deep within you and would not come
anywhere near you.

Les knew to his core that YOU were responsible for
him losing his job, deny it to others but YOU know
the truth and so did Les.

You believe Amanda is the narcissist when it's you
who fits the definition perfectly. The more "work" you
do on yourself, the sicker you become.

You believe everyone is taking advantage of Mr.
Burrman, because you are the one who is the guiltiest.
Les even guessed that you are and will always remain
on Mr. Burrmans payroll even though you work very
little. You see, JULIE, you are FOOLING NO ONE!

If you have remained on the payroll, it's because you're not qualified to be anything but the office BITCH!

I don't know you, and you certainly don't know me, as I don't have toxic people in my life. I have done some research on you and have talked to a few people who have worked under you and they have all confirmed what Les has told me and that is what makes me so angry at you. You do this by choice!!!

I'm writing this because I wanted to tell you that I lost a good friend and I HOLD YOU PARTIALLY RESPONSIBLE. You kicked a man when he was down, and I pray to God that happens to you someday.

I HOPE YOU CAN LIVE WITH THE REALITY THAT YOU CONTRIBUTED TO LES'S DEATH and now those children have to grow up without a father partially thanks to you.

My new life long prayer is that Mr. Burrman will someday see the true light and see who you REALLY ARE AND THAT IS PURE EVIL. You may think you're fooling people, but you know the truth and there is NO pretending when you look in the mirror and that does give me some relief.

I'm also contemplating giving Les's family a copy of this letter as well, guess you will never know if that happens but give it some thought.

Don't ever run for office or write a book because if I ever hear about it, I'll tell the world what I have heard about you.

Good news for you is there's one less Julie Jacky hater in this world.

Doug quietly listened, and when I finished reading, he replied. I don't think I'll ever forget what he said. "You know, I've received letters like that before. Not quite as bad as the one you got, though. You'll feel better in a couple of days."

I rolled my eyes, shook my head, and laughed; and that's exactly what he was trying to do. I had already gone into fight-flight-freeze mode, and he was trying to get me out of it. He had a funny and effective way of interrupting people when they were going into that yucky, no-good storytelling mode. I appreciated what he did for me. It was all too easy to make something horrible out of a piece of white paper with black typed words on it. But at that moment, I still felt very distraught.

"Oh, Doug, this is terrible!" I exclaimed as I shook my head in disbelief.

He replied, "Julie, you didn't have anything to do with Les's death. That's on him, not on you. You couldn't have done anything to change it."

I agreed that I didn't have anything to do with his death, but I still wondered if I could have handled things differently and if it would have changed the outcome in any way.

Doug reassured me, "No, you handled everything just fine. It's a common response people have after someone passes away to think they could have done something different to help change the other person, but you're not responsible."

I knew Doug was speaking from many years of experience, and he didn't want me to take on a burden that wasn't mine to carry. I thanked him for saying that and let him know I would let go of any other thoughts about it. Doug encouraged me to take some time to process the letter and reminded me that I would feel better in a couple of days.

After I hung up the phone with Doug, my body and mind were still freaking out on the inside. They were still in fight-flight-freeze mode. I walked across the street to the beach, took off my flip-flops, and left them in the sand near the bottom of the stairs. I walked toward the ocean. I had my phone with me and called Kim. No answer. Next, I called Patti. No answer. Then I called Kristy. She answered.

Thank God!

There was no doubt that Kristy could hear the panic in my voice, because I sounded out of breath. I told her I had received a letter that was holding me partially responsible for someone's death, and I didn't even know what to do or say. She told me to take a deep breath in and focus on opening my heart back up. Then she said, "Know you are safe, Julie."

I told her I didn't even know why someone would send a letter like that or how to start dealing with it. Her words of wisdom to me were, "Well, you know this, but I hate to say it. There's some reason that you got that letter, and you need to own whatever your stuff is in that."

"Damn it! You're right," I agreed. "Thanks a lot," I added with sarcasm.

Fucking A! She's absolutely right. When I'm triggered, it's my own crap. I gotta get to work on this. I want to clear it out and find out what is underneath it all. Fucking A! Why did this have to come today? I was feeling so good. I want to feel good again.

I let out a big sigh of resignation and exclaimed in a sarcastic tone, "Fine! I will do my work to get to a place where I find the gift in this fucking letter." And then I chuckled, knowing my tone sounded ridiculous.

After we hung up, for a good ten minutes I continued

grounding my bare feet in the warm sand and tapping on the sides of my fingertips. I then imagined my heart opening up and said, "I am safe."

I felt a little calmer. I put my flip-flops back on, walked home, and started tapping on all the main tapping points. There was a lot of work ahead to calm my body and slowly and intentionally work through every sentence in that letter. I knew that if I spoke about this situation or read the letter without tapping, my stress level would increase. So I made a promise to myself to tap every time I talked about or read the letter, period.

First, I tapped while looking at the white envelope with the black writing, and then I pulled the letter back out. I slowly opened it, and before reading any words, I noticed I felt confused and quite topsy-turvy inside. I was puzzled as to why in the world someone would send such a mean letter like that. I kept tapping through the points while paying attention to the thoughts fluttering through my head and the sensations inside my body. I could tell my body was significantly calming down. My heart wasn't racing as fast, and I didn't feel panicked inside anymore. Besides, I had a reasonable game plan, and I could tackle a little bit of the letter at a time.

My phone rang, and it was Kim. She wanted to know if I was okay, since I had called but hadn't left a message or sent a text. While still tapping, I explained to her that I had received a nasty hate letter in the mail. I didn't feel like it was right to read it to Kim because I didn't want to dump that on her. I hadn't read it to Kristy, either, for the same reason. I let her know I was doing a lot better than when I had initially called her but had a lot of work ahead of me, so I needed to go so I could keep tapping.

After we hung up the phone, I continued tapping with the intention to calm my body down even more. My body was no longer in shock over the letter, but it was still rather disturbing to me that someone was so angry that they had mailed a hateful letter to me. Even though the anonymous writer said they didn't know me, I thought I knew who wrote it: a former employee who had angrily stomped out of the family office. Later, while tapping and talking, I responded as if she had written it, which helped me get anger out about that person. But ultimately, it didn't matter who had written the letter.

And whether I knew who the writer was or not, I felt creeped out and unfairly attacked. Now that my body was calmer, I set the intention to thoroughly go through the letter to get all the emotions out. I'd found it was way more powerful to speak out loud while tapping, so that was what I did. Starting at the top of my head and continuously moving through the tapping points, I vented, "This letter is creepy. And it feels creepy that someone I don't know would have several conversations about me."

I shivered and moved on to the next tapping point. "And then confirmed it with others. Get a real hobby, for fuck's sake!" I repeated that last sentence a few times because I could hear the extra emphasis on the two last words. Each time I repeated the phrase, I switched to the next tapping point.

I continued tapping and venting because it was better to get all those crappy thoughts and feelings out than it was to leave them in. "Don't you have anything better to do than sit around and talk about me? Get a life!" I exclaimed.

It was also disconcerting to me that my new mailing address had somehow been acquired because it wasn't easily obtainable, and I hadn't given it out to many people yet. I continued venting, "And how did you get my address? Why are you stalking me? Don't you have a life of your own?" But the next moment, I also realized how easy it was to research people on the internet in addition to having conversations about them with others.

I paused my venting but kept tapping while looking back down at the letter, then read, "'You sandbag your employees. You manage in fear. All your employees were looking for jobs. Office BITCH.'"

Wow! I thought. *All that is pretty fucking intense. It sounds exactly like Les talking.* He had said some of those things to me when we'd had our conversation in the upstairs office over two years earlier. *At least he didn't call me a bitch to my face*, I thought. I shook my head in disbelief. *Why is someone writing about things from two years ago if they don't even know me?* I couldn't grasp why someone would spend time being so concerned about Les's angry assessment of my management style if they didn't even know me. It just didn't make any sense.

I googled *sandbag your employees* and read a couple of different definitions and articles that included examples of being sandbagged. I wanted to understand what I was being accused of by Anonymous. I chuckled at the irony. All the behaviors listed were ways Les treated me to divert attention away from his improper actions.

That's the pot calling the kettle black, I thought.

Looking back down at the letter and still tapping through the points, I read through the bottom half of the page that focused on blaming me for Les's behavior, like "YOU were responsible for him losing his job," "You kicked a man when he was down," and "YOU CONTRIBUTED TO LES'S DEATH." I already knew none of that was true. I didn't make Les not show up to work. I didn't make him drink or take anything that brought death to him. He did that on his own.

I did, however, feel sad that Les's life ended that way. We used to be friends, and I did care about him. I felt terrible that his children would have to grow up without their father. It sucks that any kid would have to grow up without a father. It made my heart hurt for them.

After tapping for quite a while, my phone rang again. This time, it was Patti calling me back. I continued tapping as I gave her a brief synopsis of my not-as-urgent-but-still-yucky situation. She asked me if I would like her support with tapping through the letter. Even though I was plugging away on my own and wasn't excited to share the mean-spirited messages with her, I happily took her up on her offer. I appreciated the support and knew she would catch where I was triggered by hearing it in my voice, just like she had when we had tapped on "I am worthy" and other topics after that.

I took a deep breath in and started at the beginning, and over the next two-and-a-half hours I slowly read the letter out loud to her as we continuously tapped the entire time. I read a little bit at a time, and sentence by sentence she helped me process it. She stopped me each time she heard fluctuations in my voice and helped me deep dive into the shadows of each accusation that triggered me. We did this so I could own all the parts of me that I didn't want to claim, just like Nancy Levin had taught me when I had been triggered by the word *victim*. I owned the bitch part of me, the narcissist part of me, the angry part of me. I asked what I needed to own and accept about myself. I owned every piece, because the truth is that each of us has all those parts, and we don't always like to admit that about ourselves—or at least I know I don't want to admit that crap to myself. But I understood then that I needed to work through it, and I still understand this and do my personal work today whenever it's needed.

As we continued tapping and I read the phrase, "You are a FRAUD," I was happy to report to Patti that I didn't feel like a fraud and wasn't triggered by this at all. I used to feel like a fraud because I used to be so inauthentic, especially when I had gone broke. I had put on a happy mask, pretended everything was okay when it wasn't, and focused more on others to my detriment. Back then, it had felt like I was a fraud. But as I had started doing my personal work and healing from my past, I had realized that when I didn't want to tell the truth about how I felt, that was exactly the time I needed to tell the truth. That's a must now to keep the happy mask off. Now I am more authentic every day and have better relationships as a result.

Patti and I had been tapping together a few years at this point, and she confirmed with me all the changes I had made and how different I was from when she had first met me in the EFT certification class, when I had quietly sat in the back of the room.

After further tapping, I could see that because I had done my personal work and changed myself, I may have been perceived as a threat to others even subconsciously. I had applied better communication styles by listening and asking more questions. I had become more assertive and held people more accountable for their work and behavior rather than ignoring or letting things slide until they became a problem. It had become easier for me to see their bullshit stories and excuses, and to kindly call them out on it. If they didn't like

ON THE OTHER SIDE

that, then I could see how they thought I was a bitch. Most people don't like or want to be held accountable, especially when they know they're doing something wrong.

After tapping on a few sentences, I read, "'You believe Amanda is the narcissist when it's you who fits the definition perfectly.'"

Whoa, I didn't like being called a narcissist! Patti could hear that in my voice. This letter allowed me to reflect on the word *narcissist*. I didn't think I fit the definition perfectly, but I tapped anyway. I argued with myself out loud so Patti could hear me work through being a narcissist. "I am a narcissist," I firmly stated. Then I moved to the next tapping point. "No, I'm not a narcissist!" I exclaimed.

I kept tapping through each point, arguing both sides of the debate with extra emphasis in my voice as if I meant each statement to be true, until I got clarity in my mind and shared it with Patti.

I told Patti that I wasn't proud to admit this, but there had been times in my life where I had behaved like a narcissist. Back then, I had been really into myself and hadn't paid as much attention to other people. I used to have an attitude that it was my way or the highway. That wasn't who I was anymore, nor who I'd been for a long time. That had been a defense mechanism to keep myself safe.

I continued tapping. "Plus, a narcissist wouldn't be doing personal work because they think they are better than everyone else. Clearly, I'm doing personal work right now in this moment," I exclaimed. "I have the mindset of being a steward and serving my boss. I wouldn't be able to do that if I were a narcissist."

ANONYMOUS

Frankly, I don't know anybody who likes being called a narcissist. But the truth is, all of us are capable of being one.

I moved on to the following statement. "'The more "work" you do on yourself, the sicker you become,'" I read.

I repeated the phrase while tapping a couple of rounds, and then I shared with Patti the affirming thoughts that were flooding my mind. "The more work I do on myself, the better I feel. The more confidence I have, the more I can communicate clearly with people. The more authentic I am, the more I can have difficult conversations with people, and then the more compassionate I am. Now I have more quality conversations than I've ever had before. I ask questions for clarity and understanding. In my opinion, I have become a way better person. I've become healthier, more confident, stronger, and more intuitive. Not sicker," I said as I shook my head.

At that point, I felt really good about the person I'd become as I peeled the layers back over the years. I had already decided that I was going to keep doing my personal work. This letter wasn't going to stop me. If anything, it pushed me to do *more* personal work.

I moved on to the next part and jokingly said to Patti, "But wait, there is more." Then I continued reading while tapping. "You may think you're fooling people, but you know the truth, and there is NO pretending when you look in the mirror, and that does give me some relief."

I paused a moment to collect the thoughts fluttering through my mind. "Wowza. I am not sure what I am fooling people about here, Patti. But when I look in the mirror, I love myself more than I ever had before, and that feels good to me."

I took a deep breath into my heart and sat with that for a moment. I'd come such a long way.

Interestingly, as I continued tapping, I was able to see the writer of the letter deflecting her grief and anger onto me. There was a part of me that felt bad for her because she was in so much pain that she had taken time and energy to compose that letter. I hoped that writing the letter had helped her get that nasty crap out of her body. But I knew from personal experience that there's a bit more work we have to do to take personal responsibility and process through our emotions. After my own letter-writing experiences, I had suggested to my clients that they write letters to people when they're angry or frustrated. But I had always told them to tap during the process and NEVER to send it. The point of the letter-writing exercise was to work through thoughts and emotions and to find relief after expressing them, not to demean someone by sending the angry letter to them.

I better take my own advice here and write a letter, I thought.

I jotted *write a response letter to Anonymous* in my journal and continued reading the letter out loud to Patti—while tapping, of course.

I got down to the last sentence. It felt like a vague threat to me. "'Don't ever run for office or write a book because if I ever hear about it, I'll tell the world what I have heard about you,'" I read.

That triggered me because at the time I received the letter, I had started writing a book proposal. I was going to submit it to a Hay House Writer's Workshop contest the following spring. Now I had some unknown person vaguely threatening to tell the world how horrible they thought I was even though they claimed not to know me. But I didn't want that getting in my way of writing a book. So I tapped on that too.

After tapping through that whole letter, I felt a lot better and was also exhausted and ready for bed. I thanked Patti for all her support, and we said good night.

DEAR ANONYMOUS

The next day, the letter was still on my mind, and I was determined to keep doing my personal work until I cleared everything out and felt resolved with the whole situation. I knew somehow, someway, there would be a gift at the end of my personal work, like a pot of gold at the end of a rainbow after a storm. So that evening, I sat up in my bed, pulled my journal out of my nightstand, and wrote back to Anonymous. Admittedly, when I started writing a letter back to her, the first drafts weren't very kind. They had a lot of ego in them. I was making her wrong and me right by pointing out her issues.

To start, I snobbily called her a toxic person and told her to go to her therapist. I pointed out that she was indeed toxic and needed to do her personal work. As I combined tapping into the writing process, I began to clear out my triggers and my need to make her wrong. I'm sharing the draft letter with you here so you can see the process and how my mind and heart shifted after I cleared out my own emotions.

Here's the first draft letter I wrote to Anonymous:

Dear Toxic Person who claims not to know me and writes a letter filled with anger and hatred and hearsay trying to tell me what my beliefs are and holding me partially responsible for Les Wilson's death,

Please take your letter to your therapist and have
them help you deal with your anger and hatred.

I'm sorry that you're hurting so terribly inside that
you felt the need to write a letter with hate, anger, and
venom along with negative prayers and hopes.

It's a very toxic letter, and in order for you to have
written it you must be toxic.

Sending you love.

Reading over the draft, I thought, *Oh jeez, you've got a lot
of anger and a heck of a lot of ego in there, Julie, telling her to
take her letter to her therapist. Let's tap a little more on those
judgmental thoughts and then try again.*

I flipped to the next page in my journal to start over. The
second draft letter I wrote to Anonymous was a little more
compassionate, but still had triggers I needed to work through
because I continued pointing out her shortcomings.

Dear hurting person,

I'm filled with nothing but compassion for you. You
must be deeply hurting on the inside in order to take
the time to compose hate mail and send it while
pretending to be a good Christian.

My prayer for you is that you find peace and love and
compassion for yourself and others.

I forgive you for your actions against me.

Oh, Julie, that's a little better, I thought. *But there is still a fair amount of ego in there. You are still trying to point out how she is wrong, and now you're made the assumption she's a good Christian because you think you know who wrote the letter. Try again, girlfriend.*

I flipped over another page in my journal and rewrote the letter. In fact, I rewrote it a few more times, each time removing the feeling of wanting to prove her wrong. Then I realized that all of those letters had "good Christian" in them. *Julie, you are clearly charged by the phrase "good Christian,"* I thought.

I started tapping and reflecting on the phrase *good Christian*, and a memory arose in my mind. There was a letter that I had sent to my husband's grandmother, probably a good twenty years earlier. She had treated her grandson, one of my husband's cousins, poorly. It infuriated me that she had claimed she was a good Christian yet treated her grandson very unkindly.

I recalled how unkind my letter was to her, that I didn't have both sides of the story, and that the whole situation was none of my business in the first place. It hadn't been appropriate to butt in. I tapped through my sorrow and apologized to her in my mind, letting her know I was sorry and that I realized both of us were doing the very best we could at the time. After tapping on my trigger, I understood why the letter writer might be angry and butt in to protect someone she called a friend.

In hindsight, I also saw how lashing out at someone back then could easily take attention off my need to do personal work even though I was deeply hurting inside. I felt the same for Anonymous. I saw a younger version of Julie in this situation. I genuinely felt compassion for younger Julie and Anonymous. I kept rewriting and tapping because I was deter-mined to work through all of my emotions from my past. By the time I reached my eighth draft, the letter to Anonymous was different. It was shorter. It was simpler, and it didn't make her out to be bad or wrong so I could feel right. It was also a lot more compassionate and heartfelt.

The eighth draft letter to Anonymous went like this:

My heart is filled with love and compassion for you. You must be hurting deeply. I am sorry for what you're going through and for what you've been through in the past that is causing you so much pain. My prayer for you is that you're able to find love, peace, and compassion for yourself and others.

Sincerely,

Julie

I sat there for a moment and noticed my lower back felt a lot looser. I put my right hand on my left shoulder, closed my eyes, and invited in resources from other dimensions and asked them to help loosen my shoulder. Then I heard a mes-sage that I was on the right path and to keep processing the letter.

I wrote in my journal, *I'm letting go of the letter now. God, please help me fully let go.* I laid my journal and pen on my nightstand and closed my eyes to drift off to sleep.

FORGIVING ANONYMOUS

But my rest didn't last long. I was still upset. So I got up and wrote in my journal, *So much for sleeping! I'm so wide awake right now. I just don't want to spend any more time or energy on this crap about people at the family office.*

However, since I was wide awake, it seemed like a good time to go through the steps that Mary had led me through in the forgiveness workshop when I forgave Dan. Especially since I had just requested that God help me fully let it go. I didn't expect my request to be answered immediately, but I started with getting the rest of the anger toward Anonymous out of my body. I didn't want to hang on to that anymore. My anger wasn't hurting Anonymous; it was only hurting me.

Like Mary had taught me in the forgiveness workshop, I let loose. I started a rant while tapping on the top of my head and shouted, "Fuck you, Anonymous! Fuck you, Anonymous! Who the hell are you to write to me, you crazy stalker! You're not a good person."

After several rounds of tapping over a few minutes, I let out a huge sigh and thought, *Well, that's not okay to say. She's a person making poor decisions.*

I was surprised how quickly my mind shifted to a positive place with Anonymous and how that sigh provided so much relief. I wasn't trying to be positive. I was trying to get the crap out. Then I realized I had released so many emotions toward Anonymous when I was writing the response letter and tapping.

A moment later, I had an idea of what to do for Anonymous. *I could ask friends to mail a note to her,* I thought. *It would be from a space of love with good intentions and positive vibes, and she might feel love from others instead of the hate she sent out.* For a moment, I thought that was a great idea. Her mailbox would get flooded with love, and that could help shift her to be more kind or even reflect on her own choices. But then I realized that would mean I'd have to give out her home address, and I wasn't willing to do that. It had felt invasive when I received a highly emotional letter from Anonymous. I didn't want someone else to feel invaded with multiple anonymous letters, even though they would be sent in love instead of hate.

Instead, I paused and sent love to her at that moment. I imagined a fire hose of sparkly love hearts spraying from my heart where I was sitting in Florida and shooting all the way to hers in Minnesota. Then I wrote in my journal:

I release the expectation of Anonymous changing.

I release the expectation that Anonymous will ever apologize.

I release the expectation that Anonymous will see how hurtful she has been to people.

I release the expectation that Anonymous will do her work, heal, or ever say nice things about me.

I went through the rest of the forgiveness steps, and at the end I knew I didn't need to rewrite the letter anymore. I sent more love to her and let go once and for all.

After that, I got up for a glass of water and stretched my body before I switched to focus on getting out all my anger toward Les. There was a heck of a lot of anger toward him.

Still standing, I took a deep breath in preparing to let it all out on this rant too. I reminded myself, *You can do this, Julie. You'll feel so much better afterward. Go for it!*

There was a lot more to get out because I was very angry with him for blaming crap on me the previous two years, making me out to be a bad manager, and causing so much unnecessary drama in the office.

"Fuck you, Les! Fuck you! You fucking, lying, stealing son of a bitch. You lied straight to my face so many times. You talked shit behind my back to employees. Blaming me for *your* bullshit. Fuck you."

With complete sarcasm, I continued shouting, "Oh, I get it. You were a closet alcoholic. Oh, I get it. You were probably on drugs too. Well, fuck you!"

There were a lot more fuck-yous and other unkind venting and releasing during the ranting tapping session. I let go of the grudges I held. I let go of the anger toward Les. I made myself get it all out as part of the forgiveness process, just as I had done when I had kneed the pillow to get my anger toward Dan out.

I sat back down in my chair and imagined Les sitting across from me. I repeated the process of writing down and releasing expectations, but this time for him. Even though he had passed away, this was important for me to let go of. But it did feel a little awkward talking to him now that he was gone.

I release the expectation of you taking personal responsibility.

I release the expectation of you being honest and telling the whole truth.

I release the expectation that you stop blaming me.

I release the expectation that you be kind to me.

I took a deep breath in and felt my shoulders drop and stomach calm as I let out a big sigh. Then I continued through the remaining forgiveness steps, focusing on letting go of every ill feeling I had toward Les.

After I felt complete, I paused and reflected on the good that I had received from the letter and Les. After receiving that letter, I had reached out to friends, asked for help, and received support and guidance from them in response. That was all a gift. Then I saw the gift in the triggers: I had gotten to work through so many different situations I experienced over the last eight years at the family office. That allowed me to more fully let go of my role as an employee and move into a consultant role in the new year, just as I had set the intention to do.

I also thanked Les, because had he not triggered me and blamed me over the years, I wouldn't have gotten so much practice learning to trust my intuition, having difficult conversations, and feeling as confident about my personal changes. All this had resulted in a better relationship with Doug. I had also become a better person and a better coach to my clients as a result.

As I reflected back on this experience over the next several days, I thought about what the old Julie would have done. I would have called a lot more people, read them the letter without thinking how it would have impacted them, and made Anonymous out to be a horrible Christian.

I could see how far I had come from that earlier version

of myself because I could recognize my body's behaviors and work through my emotions that I had previously been unaware of and numbed out. So when I had gone into fight-flight-freeze mode after reading the anonymous letter, I had been aware of it and able to get myself out of it by tapping and breathing.

Instead of avoiding feeling, pretending it didn't happen, or blaming someone else, I took responsibility by jumping into the crappy emotions to work through my triggers. Then I could see they were both hurt people lashing out, blaming other people and things outside them instead of taking responsibility for their own personal work. I owned what was mine, did my work, left what was theirs, and let go.

Chapter Sixteen
THE WORK CONTINUES

TEMPER TANTRUM

In the new year, just a little over a month after receiving the letter from Anonymous, I was now fully self-employed and got to structure my days how I wanted to. I scheduled writing time on my calendar for my book proposal. And as I started writing EFT stories, something felt off. I tried to figure out what it was. I noticed I had written several blogs for my website over the last few months, and I found it odd that none of them were about EFT, which was the topic of my book. Instead, they were all about personal experiences and lessons I had learned. Then when I looked at my list of topics for future blogs, I noticed they were all personal stories as well. I was more inspired to write those personal stories than blogs about tapping for some reason.

Oh my gosh, I have a feeling I'm writing the wrong book, I thought. *If this is the wrong book, then what is the right book?*

Over the next day and a half, I was intent on figuring out what the right book was. I felt compelled to put together a list of impactful experiences during five years of my life. After pondering the link between all of these stories, I saw the thread that stitched them together. The stories all stemmed from working through situations from my past to build a relationship with myself. The shifts I had made during that time were to heal and forgive after childhood sexual abuse. But now I was on the other side of the abuse after working through it.

Oh my God, I don't want to write that fucking book, I thought. *That's way too personal and vulnerable.*

But I had a clear knowing *that* was the book I was being guided to write. The book that emerged wasn't a book I had ever planned on writing, but I was being nudged to write about it. I felt energized working on the story timeline and figuring out the title.

A few weeks later, on the connecting flight from Atlanta, Georgia, to Albuquerque, New Mexico, I was on my way to another of Dr. Joe Dispenza's Advanced retreats. I nestled myself into the seat next to the window. My notebook was perched on the seat back tray, and my pen was in hand. I focused on writing stories that were going to be in my new book. I had a lot of writing to do because the day I had resigned from my job and received the anonymous letter, I had put my book proposal on hold. Now I needed to make up for lost time on my book proposal to meet the upcoming deadline to enter the Hay House Writer's Contest.

I literally wrote nonstop the whole three hours of the flight. My blue gel pen glided across pages, and my hand cramped up, but it didn't matter because I was in the flow. I wasn't going to let a little pain in my hand stop my writing process, so I shook it out, stretched my fingers, and continued on.

As I began writing this book proposal and dug out old memories to write about, it became crystal clear to me that I needed to get even more personal in my book than I had bargained for. I had absolutely no intention of talking to people or writing in my book about the taboo topic that resurfaced.

That was something I preferred to keep to myself. I jotted a reminder word in my notebook and put it out of mind until later.

After I got off the plane in Albuquerque, the taboo topic came back into my mind. I was upset. I had no intention of revisiting that time in my life. And yet I felt a force urging me to write about it. God was calling me once again.

I yelled and screamed at God for the better portion of the hour drive while on the way to my hotel in Santa Fe. I rationalized and reasoned with God that I was already writing about apologizing to my ex-husband. I was sharing that whole forgiveness process of what I went through and how it felt forgiving the person who sexually abused me. I was also going to write about the details of some of my therapy sessions. So I informed God that, since I was already sharing all that, I didn't want to write about the abortion too.

THE STORY I NEVER MEANT TO TELL

Right after my sweet sixteenth birthday, I had an abortion. I didn't want to tell anybody my deep, dark secret because I was afraid they would judge me for doing something society perceived as evil. And abortion isn't something we talk about out loud with others unless we're in a political debate, arguing against killing or for women's rights.

Most women who have shared with me that they had an abortion have also told me they were too ashamed to talk about it. They'd only told one or two people before telling me. And they carefully selected who they told so they would feel safe and wouldn't be judged. They were grateful they could share with me and found comfort and relief in doing so.

241

The problem with our society not engaging in meaningful conversations about abortions and instead shaming women for their decision is that it's counterproductive. It doesn't allow women to heal from whatever led them to have to make that decision in the first place. Shame shuts us down and makes us want to hide inside instead of opening up to work through the healing process. It adds another layer on top, and it's not a cherry.

I remember the day I was in the bathroom stall in the high school gym locker room with my friend, Salina. Something was off. I noticed my pants were tight around the waist, my belly was sticking out, and I had to go to the bathroom more frequently. It dawned on me that I could be pregnant. I was shaking and embarrassed, and today I really can't remember if I bought the pregnancy test or if a girlfriend bought it for me. But I do remember watching lines on the white stick slowly turn pink, creating a cross.

Oh my God. Oh my God. Oh my God, I slowly repeated to myself. *I can't believe this. I am pregnant. How could this happen to me? What am I going to do? My life is over. My parents are going to hate me if they find out.*

I didn't know who to trust enough to talk with about my predicament. I was afraid to talk with either of my parents. Not because they were scary, but because of all the fearful thoughts I created in my head. I didn't want to hurt, disappoint, or embarrass my parents, especially since they had adopted me into the family. I didn't want to be *that* problem child. I was terrified they would be upset with me for being a bad Catholic girl, and I felt a tremendous amount of shame.

Worse yet, I was afraid they would make me have the baby if I told them. I thought having a baby at that age would be humiliating. I didn't want to have to go to the special school for pregnant girls, druggies, and other people that were classified as misfits and could no longer attend the regular high school. I thought having a baby at that age would ruin my life, and I wouldn't be able to go to college.

I also knew I wasn't going to have the baby and give it up for adoption. This I knew for certain. I felt the impact of feeling like the black sheep in my adopted family. They didn't try to make me feel that way; it was my thoughts that made me feel it. But the fact that my birth mother had given me up for adoption when she could have made another choice meant fierce judgment upon myself if I chose to have an abortion. At times, it almost felt like I was taking the easy way out by considering having an abortion, but it sure didn't feel like an easy thing to do.

I wasn't ready to be a mother to anyone. I was just a child myself.

After several anxiety-filled days of secretly consulting with a couple of close girlfriends, I called my on-again, off-again boyfriend and blurted out that I was pregnant with his baby. I have no idea what he said to me on the phone that day. I just remember the fear and terror I felt inside about telling him I was pregnant and the possibility of having an abortion. It wasn't an easy conversation for a fifteen-year-old girl to have with her sixteen-year-old boyfriend.

After thinking about my options, one of the girlfriends who I confided in called Planned Parenthood for me. I was too afraid to make the call myself. (We didn't have internet easily accessible back then like we do now, and cell phones weren't readily available for the public yet.) She found out information about abortions, including the cost, what the process entailed, and how long it would take.

A few days later, I called to make an appointment.

The appointment day arrived. My friend and her boyfriend, Derick, dropped me off at the front of the building and then went to park his car. I slowly opened the big metal door and entered Planned Parenthood. I felt scared and ashamed as I checked in at the reception desk and sat down in a chair in the waiting room. I glanced around to look at the other women there and wondered if they were all getting abortions too. I was very anxious, and it felt like it was taking forever to get called. The lady next to me could probably see the fear in my eyes and tried to comfort me. She told me she was there for her third abortion, and I would be just fine. I was surprised she told me that, and I know I judged her. *I can understand the first one because I am in that situation,* I thought. *But why did she have a second and third abortion? Didn't she learn after the first one?*

My friends joined me in the waiting room. After what seemed like the longest wait ever, they called my name. I got up and looked at my friends, then turned to walk toward the nurse. She led me to a procedure room. She tried to make me feel as comfortable as possible as she asked me to take my clothes off and put on a gown. Then she instructed me to lie down on the padded blue plastic portion of the table. She let me know I would be okay and asked me a long list of questions. Then she provided me with information on how the process and procedure would go to make sure I fully understood what I was getting myself into and to confirm that I completely understood the procedure was not reversible. I asked her a few questions about the process and also why someone would have three abortions. She explained to me that sometimes women are put in tough situations and aren't able to have or raise their babies, whether it is because of rape, sexual abuse, or something else. I began to let go of my judgment of the woman in the waiting room.

When it was finally time for the procedure, I turned my head toward the wall, closed my eyes and squeezed them as tightly as I could, and held my breath. As the fetus was sucked out of my body and into a tube, a couple of tears leaked from my eyes and slowly rolled down my cheeks. The whole procedure was over in a matter of minutes. My body cramped up, and I could feel blood flowing from me onto the metal portion of the procedure table. The nurse helped me move off the table and down the hall to the recovery room to rest before discharging me.

On the way back to my house, Derick pulled the car over so I could open the door to throw up on the side of the road. When I arrived home and my mom questioned where I had been, I lied. Although it was true that I had thrown up on the way home, it wasn't true that the after-school bus had pulled over for me and then dropped me off. I couldn't look her in the face between the shame and the cramps. I told her I didn't feel well and went to bed.

When I woke up the next morning, I felt better. I got dressed, went to school, and pretended nothing had happened. Just like that.

The following summer, my dad asked me to go door-to-door with him to hand out pro-life flyers in support of the Catholic church and a Republican candidate who was running for president of the United States the next year. Although I wasn't in favor of killing anyone, including unborn babies, I had had an abortion and couldn't go around telling people it was wrong. I would have felt like a hypocrite. I also didn't want to go around telling people abortions were okay, even though I had just had one. It was confusing, and I felt so mixed up inside. The shame, embarrassment, humiliation, and all the other feelings I had inside of me about aborting the baby were feelings I wanted to shove way down so I wouldn't have to feel them or talk about that topic with anyone—ever.

That was the story I didn't want to share all those years later. I didn't want to tell people THAT part of my life. "Can't I just leave it out? Please, God," I pleaded during the car ride to Santa Fe. "Why do I have to share that? That's not something I want to talk to people about or even admit. Especially in a book." I was distraught that I should have to put that story in the book.

Sometimes God has a great fucking sense of humor that's also annoying. Inside my head, she said, *Well, Julie, I don't want you to write about just that one. I also want you to write about the other abortion.*

"Oh my God. Fuck you. Fuck you!" I screamed.

Julie, you didn't just have one. You had two, and you need to include both of them in the book.

"FUCK YOU! Fuck you, God! I don't want to. I don't want to include any of that in my book! I don't want to tell people that when I was nineteen, I was dating a twenty-seven-year-old and got pregnant and had a second abortion," I exclaimed.

I felt embarrassed, humiliated, shameful, and every other crappy emotion because I had not one but two abortions when I was a teen.

I yelled and screamed, "God, I don't want to write about

having one abortion, let alone two. Twice. Twice, God. Twice I had an abortion."

Still emotional, I paused for a brief moment, and when I continued, the next words that fell out of my mouth changed me. "And somehow, you still love me."

At that realization that God still loved me, I stopped screaming and started sobbing. It was sinking in that despite my choices and actions, God did still love me, and I was worthy of his love—no matter what.

Clearly, God wanted that in my book as part of my sexual abuse healing journey. God happened to have a track record of being right, and I knew God was probably right about this too. So I surrendered an angry and frustrated "I don't really want to" sort of surrender and let go. As if I had some kind of control and could tell God what to do, I shouted to God, "Fine! If you want me to put those abortion stories in the book, then you better find someone to help me heal! Because clearly, I haven't done my personal WORK!"

WHERE FREEDOM IS HIDING

Although I don't remember exactly how I got to my hotel, I arrived there safely. I checked into the hotel very late. My suite included a small kitchen, and the whole place looked a bit dumpier than the photos I recalled seeing on the website when I had booked it. The furniture and decor were dark, rustic colors; and the couch felt like my great grandmother's hard, scratchy, monkey-vomit green couch from the 1960s that I used to nap on when I was a young kid so I could avoid watching the scary soap opera on TV. Despite my disappointment with the room, I was beyond tired and went to sleep.

The next morning, I woke congested with a stuffy nose and puffy eyes. I wondered if it was from crying so hard the night before. I lifted my head off the pillow, looked over to the couch, and saw animal claw marks on the front right corner.

Oh shit! I exclaimed. *I am in a room they allow animals in. I thought I requested to be in a room they don't allow animals in. I totally forgot to mention it again when I checked in.*

As I went about my day, I forgot to request a room change. The next morning, I was standing in line at 5:30 a.m. to get in the conference room where Dr. Joe would lead us through our first meditation. I was congested again, not only from the hotel room but also from the cigarette smoke that seeped up the stairs from the hotel's casino. Although I couldn't see smoke, the smell of it impacted me.

As I waited for the doors to open, I tapped through the tapping points while focusing on the sensations of congestion so I could have some relief and be able to breathe easily during the meditation. I wasn't worried about what the other people thought of me tapping; I figured many of them attending the retreat probably knew what tapping was, and if they didn't, they'd be open to learning. I tapped until I could breathe easier and thought to myself, *I would love to clear out these allergies and sensitivities sometime this week.*

After Dr. Joe guided us through our morning meditation, we took a break, then returned for Dr. Joe's lecture and another guided meditation before lunch.

During the second meditation, I had an interesting experience. I felt like I had a high fever and was burning up so much that I had beads of sweat above my lip and on my forehead.

I was so hot that I wanted to rip off my eye mask, take my sweater off, and throw my socks across the room for some relief. I wanted to get up and leave the room. I wanted to lie down. *What the fuck is going on?* I wondered. *I don't want to be sick. The retreat is just getting started. Mind over matter, Julie. Focus on Dr. Joe. Pay attention to him and what he is saying. Mind over matter. Mind over matter.*

I felt some tingling sensations in my body, as if my arm had fallen asleep, and I wondered if God was healing me like during the forgiveness workshop. I stayed focused on what Dr. Joe was saying as best as I could, but I was also impatiently waiting for him to tell us to lie down to integrate what we experienced. I kept hearing Dr. Joe say, "Let go. Even more. Surrender." In my mind, I asked myself how I could let go even more. I wasn't quite sure how to do it, but I was willing to surrender.

I did stay upright in my chair despite the outburst of angry chatter going on in my mind. I tried moving my body to get a little more comfortable because my neck felt contorted off to the left, but it wouldn't budge. It felt like there was a force holding it in a locked position, so I left it alone instead of fighting it.

Finally, Dr. Joe directed, "Without breaking your state, lie down."

After he said that, the teammates sitting next to me slid off their chairs and down onto the floor. Then I slumped my body over to the right, lying across the empty seats. My body fell asleep, but my mind was awake and I knew what was going on in the room. I heard the calming trance music playing in the background, heard my heavy breathing, and even saw a bright white light coming down from above into my body through my head, like what had happened after I had forgiven my abuser.

Then Dr. Joe said, "When you're ready, you may open your eyes."

I opened them and noticed I felt completely fine. I wasn't hot anymore and was actually a bit cold. The sweat beads from above my lip and brow were gone. In fact, the only evidence that I had had a fever was that my bra band was still wet because I had been sweating so much. Otherwise, I felt good.

Okay. I thought. *This is really odd. I just had an intense fever, and now I feel totally fine.*

I was confused. My logical mind couldn't quite grasp what had just happened and couldn't make sense of it. I hadn't heard anyone talk about this type of thing happening and wanted some clarity. I waited until most of my team members left the room so I could speak with our team leader about it.

She nonchalantly replied, "Oh, that happens sometimes. You were shifting a lot of energy."

That's it? I questioned to myself. *Do I need to make a bigger deal out of this? Does she understand? Is she blowing me off? I had a really intense fever!*

She didn't express the amount of concern I thought she should express, and I felt like I had to really emphasize to her how hot I had been.

To that, she simply replied, "Yeah, that happens sometimes."

I hadn't heard of that before. It wasn't like they had put in the description on the website, "You might get sick while you're on the retreat. It will be okay. Click here to sign up." That would have probably stopped people from signing up, and not everyone will experience the same thing.

That night I slept well, and when I woke up the next morning the first thing I noticed was that I could breathe easily. I didn't have any congestion. No runny nose, and the sneezing had stopped.

My logical mind connected the dots. *Huh . . . this is interesting. I am not congested this morning. I wonder if my body healed. Oh my gosh, when I was standing in line tapping yesterday morning, I thought it would be nice to clear out allergies and sensitivities sometime while I was at the retreat. That is really an intention I set and didn't realize it. I got that high fever, then I felt fine at the end of the meditation, and now I can breathe easily. I think all that hot, sweaty, high fever stuff was my body healing the allergies. Oh my gosh. This is so cool! I did experience a healing!*

It's not like I received a message in my ear saying, "Hey, we're doing a healing on your sensitivities and allergies right now. You may get a little uncomfortable, but sit still and don't worry. We will take care of everything for you, and you'll feel a lot better when you wake up in the morning."

That wasn't quite how it worked. It was a matter of putting the puzzle pieces together to understand what had taken place. The rest of the week, I didn't have any congestion. When I returned home from the retreat to my kitties, my sensitivities to them had reduced significantly too.

At lunch that day, I sat with a group and shared my experience of having a high fever and that my allergies and sensitives seemed to be gone. Then I said out loud with complete sincerity, "As much as that sucked, if I had to go through that again to experience another healing, I would."

After lunch, I found a quiet space to myself to continue journaling. This time I wrote about the realization I was having around my stomach holding the emotions from the sexual abuse, issues with men, and the two abortions. It was all right there. I understood how the messy mixture of emotions and the different areas of my life were all intertwined together. They had impacted my health.

That evening, before Dr. Joe started the meditation, he asked us once again to commit to staying in the room for the whole meditation. I never understood why someone would get up and leave. So as I had previously done, I agreed out loud that I would stay.

Dr. Joe guided us through another seated meditation. The problem was, my stomach was feeling wonky. I couldn't comfortably stay sitting, so I laid down and squirmed side to side, trying to get comfortable. I tried to stay focused on the meditation and whispered to myself, "Mind over matter, Julie. Just breathe. Mind over matter." I was trying to be quiet, but I'm sure other people could hear me because they were all in silence. I was struggling. At one point, I asked God to please help me. My stomach was agitated and felt twisted and queasy. I was doing my absolute darndest to keep my agreement and stay in the room. I wanted to stay, but I got to a point where I knew I had to get up. Most people were lying on the floor at this point, and I carefully navigated through people's bodies to not step on anyone as I made my way through the dimly lit room to the door. I was nervous. I wasn't sure if I would make it in time. When I got to the door, one of Dr. Joe's team leaders was standing there and asked me where I was going. I told her I had to throw up. She opened the door and guided me to sit on the couch to the left just outside the door. I told her again I had to throw up, and I headed toward the bathroom.

I didn't make it.

I couldn't hold it in or temporarily stop the throw-up despite trying, and I threw up all over the carpeted hallway floor at the Hilton. It flew out of my mouth with such intensity that not only did I throw up, but I also shit my pants. With my mind focused on getting to the bathroom, I stepped around the circle of chunks splattered on the floor. I was determined to make it to the toilet before anything more came out of my body.

But I didn't make it again.

I threw up another large circle of splattered chunks on the carpet.

Holy cow, there is a lot of puke, I thought. *Oh, there is my lunch. It tasted better the first time around,* I joked.

I looked up to head toward the bathroom and saw one of my favorite mentors in the whole world coming toward me.

Oh my God, I thought. *Dr. Joe is walking toward me! Talk about embarrassing. This is not good timing. I just threw up and shit my pants. What am I going to say to him? I hope he can't smell it.*

I said something super-profound. "Hey, Dr. Joe, I just threw up."

He calmly replied, in a comforting manner, "That's okay. It happens sometimes."

I also had my period and was thrilled I had put on a pad for extra protection that morning. It had saved me from further embarrassment! I pulled the shit-covered pad off my underwear and, to my delight, revealed completely clean cotton material.

After I got the barf splatter cleaned off my pants and shoes, I waited in a chair outside the meditation room directly across from the bathroom. When the meditation was over and the conference room doors reopened, I gathered my items and let some team members know I had thrown up and needed to leave. On the twenty-minute drive back to the hotel, I begged God to help me make it to my room. I was literally begging God to help me the whole twenty minutes back to my hotel.

I did make it—just in time.

Over the next day and a half, I slept a few hours, then woke up with soaking wet pajamas, went back to sleep, and woke up to soaking wet pajamas again. Each time I woke up, I checked to see how I was feeling and if I could go back to the retreat. In the late afternoon, I woke up feeling better. I was so excited that I hopped into the shower, and when I was done getting ready I was utterly exhausted and knew I didn't have enough energy to drive back to the Hilton. I laid back down and woke a few hours later, knowing I needed to stay in bed and miss out on the evening activity too. The next morning, I slept in past the walking meditation. When I woke, I finally felt like I had enough energy to drive back to the retreat.

While I was getting ready, I thought about the abortions. "Yep, that happened," I said, and nothing more.

When I arrived back into the conference room at the Hilton, Dr. Joe was talking about emotions. He said, "Whenever we have emotions, we are living in the past because it's emotions from a past experience. As we overcome those emotions by completely feeling them and moving through them, then we can let go and move forward. Things in life are still going to come up for you to deal with. We know this. But it's how long you react and how you deal with it that matter. When stuff comes up for me, I still react but not for long, and then I say 'Yeah, that just happened,' and I don't get all worked up."

The light bulb lit up in my mind as I made a connection about my experience over the past few days.

Oh my gosh, I thought excitedly. *His words—"Yeah, that just happened"—are what I said this morning about having those two abortions.* I paused as my mind made the next connection. *Throwing up in the hall helped me heal all the shame, humiliation, embarrassment, and self-judgment I had been carrying about abortion since I was sixteen. And I threw up not once, but twice. Once for each abortion.*

I was excited about my understanding of my experience, so I shared it with a couple of women during the break. One cute older lady whom I guessed to be in her sixties looked me right in the eyes and said, "Julie, thank you so much for sharing that with me. I had an abortion too. I have never talked about it with anybody because of all the shame."

Her sharing that with me helped me understand my experience even more. I knew I needed to experience that healing to be able to write about it in my book. And I realized that my personal experience of having two abortions needed to be in my book because there are so many women who, like me, have kept it a secret deep inside for not just years, but decades. Like me, they haven't felt safe to talk about abortions because of all the shame that politics and religion have put on the topic. We do need to talk about it so we can heal. We need to know we're not alone. We need comfort and empathy from others so we can stop thinking we're bad, not enough, and not worthy.

Society has turned abortion into a no-win debate and an argument without room for a compassionate conversation. And I would venture to guess some of the most influential male arguers probably have a wife, daughter, sister, niece, or mother in their life who experienced abortion too, but they won't tell him because of his loud, opinionated voice. Or maybe he knows but doesn't want to deal with his own emotions toward the experience.

Even though our society has troubles engaging in calm abortion conversations, the truth is that abortion impacts all of us way more than we're willing to admit or talk about. That's true for both men and women.

Abortion statistics estimated in the United States are likely understated because not all abortion providers are known. Only 58 percent of queried providers actually responded to the Guttmacher Institute's most recent survey. The states of California, Maryland, and New Hampshire don't publically report abortion totals. With the information provided, guesstimates were made to fill in the information gaps. Approximately 879,000 abortions took place in the United States in 2017, according to the US abortion statistics on the website Abort73. com. Globally, there are nine countries known to have higher abortion rates than the US; and despite what we may have been led to think and believe about the number of teen abortions performed, the percentages are low. Women between the ages of fifteen and nineteen accounted for less than 10 percent of abortions.

The thing is, we numb out so we don't have to feel. We do it through different means such as drugs, alcohol, food, shopping, gambling, and working too much. Those eventually get out of control and backfire, which makes it doubly hard to heal. Now we have to deal with the addiction issue and the original trauma.

As much as I didn't want to talk about abortion in my book, I know it's a part of my sexual abuse story and part of the sexual abuse stories of many others too. I know I wouldn't have had sex with as many guys as I did had I not been abused. I was an emotionally immature fifteen-year-old struggling to fit into a world where I felt like a black sheep. It wasn't the person who was abusing me that impregnated me; it was my boyfriend at the time. But had I not been abused, I now know I wouldn't have gotten pregnant. I would have had better boundaries and would have been able to speak up for myself and say no. And that is why I'm not okay with people in the name of politics and religion trying to shame or control me for being human and making the choices I made and the decision millions of other women have made.

One of the best things I've done in my life is embarking on this healing and forgiveness journey. I ventured in, out of desperation, to stop the old memories and constant chatter from further taking over my mind. I knew there was something more to life, and I was longing for it. I didn't want to do the work of dredging up my past or telling anyone my deepest, darkest secrets. But I knew from the EFT experiences I had and that first time onstage sharing my story about being broke that there's relief on the other side, and I for sure wanted more of that feeling of relief.

Through this journey, I've also learned the healing process is never-ending. There will always be more to uncover, and I have to keep working on it. I know, without a doubt, that it's essential to continue to dig in deep, and even deeper, especially when I don't want to. When I acknowledge the dark sides of my past, I regain the strength and power I wasn't even aware I had lost. And my energy restores.

The exact stories I didn't want to admit or speak aloud to myself or to others were the very stories that set me free when I told them. Speaking our truth does set us free. I've also learned that there are no shortcuts, and therefore it's wise to leave no stone unturned. I had to push myself way beyond my comfort zone; and every time I did (and still do), I became kinder, more compassionate, more loving, and grateful to both myself and others. And as a result of all the work I've done, I'm better able to serve my clients. I've started designing the life and lifestyle I want to live, and I've been cultivating authentic relationships with people I want to spend time with.

Life is way better on the other side of the pain because, ironically, that's where freedom is hiding.

When would *now* be a good time to start taking personal responsibility for your life and doing your personal work?

Chapter Seventeen

LETTER TO READER

DEAR SWEET LADY

You know it's not happenstance that you're reading this, right? Both this book and this letter are written especially for you, to let you know you're on the right path, and it's your time. Yep, you're right—there's something more to this thing called life. You've been searching for a while now because you can feel the restless yearning inside of you. That is your soul, and it has a deep desire for you to take steps to open your heart, heal, and truly be in authentic relationships with yourself and others.

I hope that, as you read my story, you began to see your own story of how trauma has permeated every aspect of your life, and that it gives you hope and inspiration to make your personal changes.

As you embark on your healing journey, you need to know that no matter what your story is, no matter what you've been through, no matter what you've done, and no matter who hurt you, it's not your fault you were sexually abused. It wasn't your fault back then and isn't your fault now.

You may not like to hear or want to believe what I have to say next, but it is key to your healing. Even though it's not your fault you were abused, *it is your responsibility to heal from your pain*, no matter who caused it. Let me repeat that so you can let it sink in. It *is* your responsibility to heal from your pain, no matter who caused it.

You may be upset and want to yell that your situation is different and no one understands. You may want to blame or even have a temper tantrum like I did with God about my two teen abortions. Go ahead and get upset—it's all part of the process. But please don't stay there. You have to let go of the anger and pain, just like I did when I kneed the pillow during the forgiveness process. Keep digging in to feel and release more, to move forward, and to help yourself heal from your past.

Freedom is waiting for you on the other side.

It's time to get started. After all, what's the alternative? Staying stuck in life, having mediocre relationships that end in hurt, and not performing work that fills you up? Continuing to say yes when, deep down inside, you want to say no, while simultaneously saying no to the things you desire? Enough already! When is now a good time to get started on your healing journey?

You may feel overwhelmed like I first did, and you may be wondering where to start. I recommend tapping to start calming your nervous system down. From there, the process is different for everyone. But let me help you by inviting you on a self-discovery path to truly get to know yourself and release the past from holding you back.

In addition to connecting with me at juliejacky.com, on the next several pages you'll find some options and resources to help you get started. Your path is unique, so tune in and get honest with yourself so you can determine what your next right step is.

Sending you oodles of love and sunshine,

Julie Jacky

P.S. Remember, it's not a one-and-done or quick-fix type of process. It's something that takes time and determination, as well as a willingness to heal and a strong desire to keep doing the work to get to the other side. Please be gentle, kind, and loving to yourself along the way.

P.P.S. You are not alone. You are loved. I am here.

RESOURCES

I chose to share the below resources with you because they offer a variety of options for you. Some of the resources are for free; and some have fees associated with them, as you might expect. It's really important for you to note that if you don't have a lot of money, please don't make that your excuse for staying stuck. There are tons of resources available for free or at a low cost to help you get started. You just need to start digging in, searching, and looking for them, and then trust that the perfect ones will be presented to you.

RAINN
RAINN (Rape, Abuse & Incest National Network) has been around for over twenty-five years and is available to help you figure out the next steps to take on your healing journey. They have a plethora of resources on their website. Some of them are free, while other links on their site connect you to resources that have a fee.

For immediate help, call RAINN's National Sexual Assault Hotline at 1-800-656-4673. They are available 24/7/365.

National Suicide Prevention Lifeline
Call 1-800-273-8255 for free confidential support. You can also go to their website, suicidepreventionlifeline.org, to get help via an online chat and to read their FAQs.

Helpful Book

The Courage to Heal: A Guide for Women Survivors of Child Sexual Abuse by Ellen Bass and Laura Davis has a lot of great information and a substantial resource section in the back. The book focuses on recovery for women who were sexually abused as children. The book was extensively updated for its second edition.

Therapist

Find a therapist who specializes in sexual abuse trauma and is trained in EMDR. If you live in the US and have insurance, you can call your insurance company to ask for help with finding a therapist near you that meets that criteria. Make sure the therapist has the EMDR designation. You'll need more tools and techniques to help you delve deeper and heal faster than traditional talk therapy alone.

You can also search for qualified therapists via RAINN (rainn.org), the American Association for Marriage and Family Therapy (aamft.org), and Psychology Today (psychologytoday. com).

MENTORS WHO HELPED ME

As I mentioned in this book, I've worked with several different mentors over the past twenty-plus years. The mentors below significantly impacted me on my journey, so I want to share their information with you.

Dr. Joe Dispenza

Dr. Joe is a researcher, educator, bestselling author, and more. He teaches tools and techniques as well as the science behind them to help people change their lives. He leads multiple week-long retreats each year where he teaches and guides participants to do the work. By doing the work he teaches, I've had so many transformational experiences in addition to the "message in the meditation" and healings I experienced at his Advanced retreats. I'm grateful for all that he went through to get to where he is today.

You can watch interviews, workshops, and testimonials on Dr. Joe's Youtube channel (drjoedispenza). The book *Breaking the Habit of Being Yourself* is a great place to start with his work. His website, drjoedispenza.com, has a plethora of resources.

Bo Eason

Bo is a former NFL player, acclaimed Broadway playwright and performer, and international story coach. Since Bo was a young boy, he has focused on and poured everything into being his best. Now he teaches others to do the same. I attended Bo's three-day Personal Story Power workshop, which provided an experience for me to learn the importance of opening up. I use that experience over and over in my life to push me out of my comfort zone in order to be my best.

Bo is also the author of the book *There's No Plan B for Your A-Game*. You can find out more about Bo and his book at his website, boeason.com.

Mary Hayes Grieco

Mary is a spiritual teacher and author who is also the director and lead trainer of the Midwest Institute for Forgiveness Training. She facilitated the forgiveness workshop I attended and guided me through all eight steps of the forgiveness process. It was a life-changing experience that I'm forever grateful for, and it gave me the desire to forgive everyone. I purchased her book *Unconditional Forgiveness* and use it to guide me through the process.

You can find that book and others as well as Mary's workshops and so much more on her website, maryhayesgrieco. com.

Nancy Levin

Nancy is a Master Integrative Life Coach and bestselling author. She helped me in so many ways over several years. I started with her book *Jump . . . and Your Life Will Appear* and progressed along a path participating in group and one-on-one coaching sessions. Nancy is real, continues to do her work, and guides others to dig in to do theirs too.

A great place to start is with the book *Jump . . . and Your*

Life Will Appear. You can find information about Nancy's other books and programs on her website, nancylevin.com.

Ann Romberg

Ann is a leadership coach and equine guided education specialist located in the Twin Cities area of Minnesota. She helped me better understand boundaries, have more awareness of my thoughts, and speak from my heart with love instead of from my head with logic.

If you're not located in the Twin Cities, then search Google for "Certified Equine Guided Educator" to find a horse coach nearest to you.

You can reach Ann through her website, carrotcoach.com.

Dr. Paul Scheele

Paul is the CEO of Scheele Learning Systems and the co-founder of Learning Strategies. He has created numerous personal learning courses and is the author of multiple books. His Ultimate You Retreat helped me understand and put into practice some of the innate powers of our subconscious minds through a variety of activities, exercises, and conversations I still call upon regularly in my life.

You can learn more about Paul and his personal learning courses at scheelelearning.com and learningstrategies.com.

GRATITUDE

I am so grateful for all the people in my life who have supported me on my journey.

I wouldn't be here and have these stories to share with you if it weren't for my mom, dad, birth mother, and birth father. Thank you for telling me I am special and for loving me no matter what.

Thank you to my sweet friends Kristy Conlan, Patti Hanson, Wendy Vaidic, Kari Doering, Ann Burns, Dr. Angie Elliot, Kim Julen, Nancy Canning, Elaine Welsh, Jeanne Barreira, Blair Shackle, Cynthia Ekren, Dorena Kohrs, Bev Kim, Erik Kim, Chara Rodriguera, Heather Nardi, Elda Dorothy, Tracy Phillips, Karen Donaldson, Brooke Emery, Niki Doering, Heather Haigh, Paula Lawrence, Laura Vasallo, and Claudine Paille for believing in me, cheering me on, checking in with me regularly, and supporting my writing process. You helped me open my heart to fully tell my story and keep going, especially on the extra-tough days. Thank you.

Doug Burrman, my boss and my mentor, thank you for investing in me and encouraging me to take on all the goddamned opportunities for personal growth that presented themselves to me. I am very grateful for you. Thank you doesn't seem like enough.

269

To my mentors Dr. Joe Dispenza, Bo Eason, Mary Hayes Grieco, Nancy Levin, Ann Romberg, Paul Scheele, Dave Ramsey, Rhonda Britten, Tony Robbins, Brendon Burchard, Brene Brown, Oprah Winfrey, Jessica Ortner, Esther Hicks, Louise Hay, Dr. Wayne Dyer, and my therapist Penny, thank you for doing your personal work before me and for teaching others to do the same. I am grateful for you, all the challenges you've overcome, and your leadership. You have helped me and positively impacted my life way more than you know. Thank you.

To my amazing book team who supported, guided, and helped me bring my book to life. First and foremost Wise Ink Creative Publishing: You flipping rock, Dara Beevas, Patrick Maloney, and Graham Warnken! Thank you for guiding me and supporting me as I followed my intuition every step of the process. Thanks to my editors: Cole Nelson, who asked me the perfect questions to help me be a better writer and connect with my reader on a deeper level, and Sara Letourneau, who beautifully and gently suggested changes to enhance my stories, To my book cover designer, Emily Mahon—I love the feeling of freedom you created. To my attorney, Aaron Hall, thank you so much for your wise counsel. My heart is bursting with love I feel for each of you for helping me on this journey.

To my ex-husband, Dave, I am sorry. Please forgive me. Thank you for loving me despite me not being able to love myself.

To my son, Craig, you may not realize that if it weren't for you, I wouldn't be who I am today. You pushed me, stretched me, and inspired me to continue to strive to be my best in ways I never could have without you. Thank you. I love you.

And last but not least, to my brothers, John and Joe, thank you for putting up with me as your little sister, for pushing me to be a better person, and for appreciating the fabulous lady I have become.

With so much love and gratitude,

Julie

ABOUT THE AUTHOR

Julie Jacky is a mindset coach and is certified as both an Emotional Freedom Technique (EFT) practitioner and a financial coach with over twenty years of business experience.

A self-proclaimed self-help and tapping geek, Julie has immersed herself in a bajillion coaching programs, workshops, trainings, and spiritual retreats over a twenty-year period on her quest to becoming the best version of herself. Now she coaches and teaches others what she has learned so they too can be the best version of themselves.

Julie loves living in Florida near the Atlantic Ocean. You can learn more about her online at juliejacky.com